MATHS & SCIENCE SERIES *2012*

MATHS
ACTIVITY BOOK

HARRY SMITH

Cisco – official Network Infrastructure supporter of the London 2012 Olympic and Paralympic Games

www.mathsandscience2012.co.uk

Go online for the interactive editions of both the Maths and Science Activity Books, along with video clips and other features.

- Open access – no registration required
- Interactive editions hosted on our ActiveTeach platform (see page 11)
- Video interviews with Olympic Competitors
- Worksheets and answers
- Details of our Maths and Science Challenge 2012 (see page 11)

Published by the Pearson Foundation, Halley Court, Jordan Hill, Oxford, OX2 8EJ

Printed in the UK by Scotprint

www.mathsandscience2012.co.uk

Acknowledgements

The authors and publisher would like to thank the following individuals and organisations for permission to reproduce photographs:

(Key: b-bottom; c-centre; l-left; r-right; t-top)

Adam Wilson: 56cr, 57tl; **Aga Khan Trust for Culture:** Michael Pearce Partnership 64tr; **Alamy Images:** Aliki Sapountzi / Aliki Image Library 17r, Bob Daemmrich 15bl, INTERFOTO / Personalities 27cr; **Alex Harvie:** 62c; **Courtesy of Cisco Systems, Inc. Unauthorised use not permitted.:** 4, 7, 12, 61t; **Copyright of Olympic Park Legacy Company, 2011:** 58-59; **Corbis:** Dallas Morning News / Tom Fox 20-21, epa / Daniel Dal Zennaro 52bl, epa / Frank May 18-19, Paul Riddle / VIEW 21tl, Peter Andrews / Reuters 24cl, Raymond Reuter 61c, Xinhua Press / Wang Song 24-25; **D-Wave Systems Inc.:** 63cl; **Eton College Rowing Centre:** 28bl; **Getty Images:** AFP 33tr, AFP / Daniel Grace 22-23, AFP / Frank Fife 48-49, AFP / Lluis Gene 48cl, AFP / Mark Ralston 42-43, Andrew Wong 16-17, Cameron Spencer 38-39, Dean Mouhtaropoulos 62cr, Feng Li 28-29, James Squire 23tl, Phil Water 44-45, Popperfoto 26cl,

Tom Shaw 20cl, 52-53; **Lee Valley Regional Park Authority:** 37tr, Philip Vile / Visit Britain 34cr; **London 2012:** 11, 22cl, 26-27, 30bl, 30-31, 34bl, 39c, 44cl, 50-51, 54cl, 54-55, 56bl, 58cr, Anthony Charlton 32cl, 34-35, 35tr, 59cr, Dave Tully 32cr, David Morley Architects 18bl, 18br, Getty Images 56-57, Steve Bates 35cr; **No Magnolia TV:** 63t; **Polymer Vision:** 63b; **POPULOUS:** 32-33; **Press Association Images:** 36-37, AP 42br, 48br, AP / Kework Djansezian 40-41, AP / Matt Dunham 14-15, Ian Nicholson 59tr, LANDOV / Jeff Siner 46-47; **Rex Features:** Associated Newspapers / Andy Hooper 49cr, 62cl; **Science Photo Library Ltd:** David Nunek 63cr, GIPhotoStock 60b, Sebastian Kaulitzki 61b; **Shutterstock.com:** Atti Tibor 45, Darren Baker 60t, EcoPrint 64cr, elsar 62t, goldenangel 46bl, JIANG HONGYAN 15cr, marcello farina 21tr, Martin Fowler 36tl, Patrick Wang 53tr, Pete Saloutos 47, Rachael Grazias 60c, RTImages 48cr, Zacarias Pereira da Mata 40br

All other images © Pearson Foundation

This project has been proudly supported by the **Pearson Foundation**. The Pearson Foundation is committed to promoting education and partners with leading nonprofit, civic and business organisations to provide financial, organisational and publishing assistance across the globe. The Foundation aims to make a difference by promoting literacy, learning, and great teaching.

The publisher gratefully acknowledges the contribution of the **Ellen MacArthur Foundation** in supporting this publication. The Ellen MacArthur Foundation is a registered charity with the aim of inspiring a generation to re-think, re-design and build a positive future. www.ellenmacarthurfoundation.org

The publisher gratefully acknowledges the contribution of the **Happold Trust** in supporting this publication. The Happold Trust is a charity established by Buro Happold Consulting Engineers to promote education, research and training in all areas relating to the built environment.

The publisher gratefully acknowledges the contribution of the **Lee Valley Regional Park Authority** in supporting this publication.

Disclaimer

The author and publisher have made every effort to ensure that this book is factually correct at the time of writing. However, due to the nature of an event such as London 2012, some details will be subject to change.

CONTENTS

CONTENTS AT A GLANCE

1 VENUES IN THE OLYMPIC PARK

Take a tour of the Olympic Park with the maths activities in this book.

Stratfo
Internat
Statio

Athletes' Village

Loop Road

BMX Circuit

Eton Manor

Velodrome

Basketball Arena

A12

River Lee

Hockey

Hockey warm–up area

Handball Arena

International Broadcast Centre/ Main Press Centre

Hackney

NETWORK INFRASTRUCTURE

During the London 2012 Games, there could be more than 200 000 people in the Olympic Park at any time, texting, tweeting and checking the latest results on their phones.

On top of that, thousands of officials, journalists, security officers and athletes need to be able to communicate quickly and reliably.

Cisco, which is the official network infrastructure supporter for London 2012, has networked more than 100 locations for the London 2012 Games, making sure that everyone can stay in touch and stay connected.

Outdoor wireless access points like this one can withstand winds of up to 165 mph.

4

Synchronised Swimming
Transformations

Diving
Formulae

Stratford City

Newham

Stratford High Street

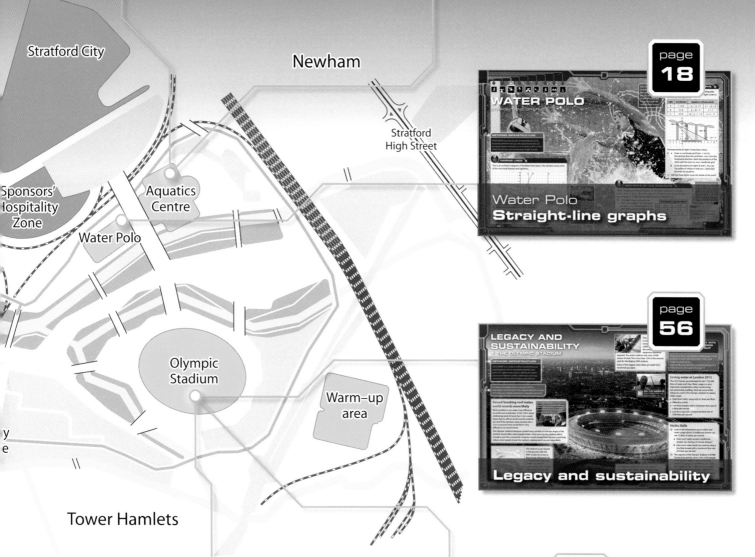

Sponsors' Hospitality Zone

Aquatics Centre

Water Polo

Olympic Stadium

Warm–up area

Tower Hamlets

Water Polo
Straight-line graphs

Legacy and sustainability

100 m Sprint
Number skills 1

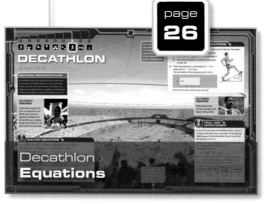

Decathlon
Equations

2 VENUES OUTSIDE THE OLYMPIC PARK

Check out some of the London 2012 venues around London and the rest of the UK with these maths activities.

Hampden Park

St James' Park

N

Old Trafford

City of Coventry Stadium

Lee Valley White Water Centre

Millennium Stadium

Eton Dorney   London

Hadleigh Farm

Brands Hatch

Weymouth and Portland

page
42

Marathon
Probability

page
48

Gymnastics
Solving angle problems

Olympic Park

Wembley Arena

Wembley Stadium

Lord's Cricket Ground

Hyde Park

The Mall

North Greenwich Arena

ExCeL

Earl's Court

Horse Guards Parade

Royal Artillery Barracks

Greenwich Park

Wimbledon

Hampton Court

page
16

Paralympic Archery
Circles

page
38

Beach Volleyball
Area and volume

page
52

Pentathlon
Averages and range

LIVE SITES

During the 2012 Games, 20 big screens will be in operation throughout the country, showing news, highlights and live action from London 2012.

20-foot LCD screens will mean spectators can be right at the heart of the action and excitement.

Supported by Cisco, these sites were just one of the ideas which organisers of the Vancouver 2010 Winter Games shared with London 2012.

Spectators in Belfast enjoy big screen tennis action live from Wimbledon.

Edinburgh

Belfast

Middlesbrough

Leeds

Bradford

Derby

Manchester

Leicester

Birmingham

Norwich

Coventry

London – Waltham Forest

Swansea

London – Woolwich

Cardiff

Dover

Portsmouth

Plymouth

Swindon

Bristol

Live Site locations in the UK. Which one is nearest to you?

SPECIFICATION MATCHING CHART

PAGES	EVENT / MATHS TOPIC		MATHS CONTENT	ENGLAND	
				AQA B	EDEXCEL A
14–15	**100 m SPRINT** Number skills 1		Fractions, decimals, mixed numbers, fractions and percentages of quantities	N1.2, N2.1, N2.2, N2.3, N2.6	Na, Nh, Ni, Nj, No
16–17	**PARALYMPIC ARCHERY** Circles		Circumference and area of circles, area and perimeter of compound shapes	G1.5, G4.1, G4.3	GMi, GMz, GMx
18–19	**WATER POLO** Straight-line graphs		Equations and gradients of lines, $y = mx + c$, coordinate grids in all four quadrants, midpoints of line segments	N6.3, N6.4, N6.11	Ak, Al, Ar
20–21	**DIVING** Formulae		Rearranging and substituting numbers into formulae, following a rule	N4.2, N5.4, N5.6	Ab, Ad, Af
22–23	**CYCLING** Representing data		Stem-and-leaf diagrams, mean and range, scatter diagrams, frequency polygons	S2.5, S3.2, S3.3, S4.1, S4.3	SPe, SPg, SPh, SPi, SPk
24–25	**SAILING** Maps and bearings		Three-figure bearings, distances, scale drawings	G3.1, G3.6	GMm, GMr
26–27	**DECATHLON** Equations		Solving equations, writing equations, sum of angles in triangle = 180°, area of rectangles, trial and improvement	N5.1, N5.4, N5.8	Ac, Ad, Ah
28–29	**ROWING** Speed and compound measures		Speed, distance and time, other compound measures	G3.4, G3.7	GMp, GMs
30–31	**MEDIA CENTRE** Ratio and proportion		Ratio, dividing a quantity in a given ratio or fraction, using percentages, direct proportion	N3.2, N3.3, **N3.3h**	Np, Nt, **Nn**
38–39	**BEACH VOLLEYBALL** Area and volume		Area of rectangles and compound shapes made from rectangles and triangles, volume, density	G4.1, G4.4	GMx, GMaa
40–41	**CANOE SPRINT** Collecting data		Suitable and unsuitable questions, two-way tables, simple probability, designing a questionnaire	S2.2, S2.3, S2.4, S3.1	SPb, SPc, SPd, SPf
42–43	**MARATHON** Probability		Simple probability, independent events, identifying all possible outcomes	S5.2, S5.7, S5.8	SPn, SPo, SPs, SPt
44–45	**BMX** Pythagoras' theorem		Pythagoras' theorem in 2D, properties of triangles and quadrilaterals, coordinates in all four quadrants, line segments	G1.4, G2.1, N6.3	GMd, GMg, Ak
46–47	**SYNCHRONISED SWIMMING** Transformations		Translations, vectors, rotations, reflections, equation of mirror line	G1.7	GMl
48–49	**GYMNASTICS** Solving angle problems		Angles in parallel and intersecting lines, triangles and quadrilaterals, sum of interior angles of regular polygons	G1.2, G1.3	GMb, GMc
50–51	**PARALYMPIC ROAD CYCLING** Real-life graphs		Drawing and interpreting conversion graphs (including non-linear), distance-time graphs, speed	N6.12, G3.7	As, GMs
52–53	**PENTATHLON** Averages and range		Median, modal class, mean, grouped data, comparing averages, frequency tables	S3.3, S4.4	SPh, SPl
54–55	**ENERGY CENTRE** Number skills 2		Percentage increase and decrease, estimation, solving percentage problems, compound measures	N2.6, N2.7, G3.7	Nm, No, GMs

OCR A	WALES WJEC	N. IRELAND CCEA	SCOTLAND CFE	STANDARD GRADE	EVENT / MATHS TOPIC	PAGES
A2.1; B2.1, 3.1, 3.3, 3.4, 3.6; C2.1	N	T1, T2, T3	MTH 4-07b	G, C	**100 m SPRINT** Number skills 1	14–15
B9.2; C2.2, 9.1	G	T1, T2, T5	MNU 3-11a,b, MNU 4-11a, MTH 4-16b	G	**PARALYMPIC ARCHERY** Circles	16–17
A6.3; B5.3, 6.1. 6.3; C5.3, 7.1	A	T1, T2, T3, T5	MTH 4-13b,c,d	G, C	**WATER POLO** Straight-line graphs	18–19
A6.2, 7.1; B5.2; C5.2	A	T1, T2, T5	MTH 3-20b, MTH 4-20b	F, G	**DIVING** Formulae	20–21
A13.3; B11.1	S	T1, T2, T3	MTH 4-20b, MTH 4-21a	F, G	**CYCLING** Representing data	22–23
A11.1	G	T1, T2	MTH 3-17b	F, G, C	**SAILING** Maps and bearings	24–25
A8.1, 8.2; C6.1, 6.2	A	T1, T2	MTH 3-15a,b, MTH 4-14a, MTH 4-15a	G	**DECATHLON** Equations	26–27
A9.1; B8.1; C4.4, 8.1	G	T2, T5	MNU 3-10a, MNU 3-11a, MNU 4-10b, MNU 4-11a	C	**ROWING** Speed and compound measures	28–29
A4.1, 4.2; B3.1; C1.1, 4.3	N	T2, T4, T5	MNU 3-08a, MNU 4-08a	G, C	**MEDIA CENTRE** Ratio and proportion	30–31
A2.2; B3.6; C4.4, 8.1, 9.1	G	T1, T2, T5	MNU 3-11a,b, MNU 4-11a	F, G	**BEACH VOLLEYBALL** Area and volume	38–39
A13.1, 13.2; C10.1	S	T1, T2, T5	MTH 3-20b, MNU 3-22a	G	**CANOE SPRINT** Collecting data	40–41
C10.1	S	T5	MNU 3-22a, MNU 4-22a	G, C	**MARATHON** Probability	42–43
A6.3, 12.1; B5.3, 9.2; C5.3	G	T1, T2	MTH 4-16a, MTH 4-18a	F, G	**BMX** Pythagoras' theorem	44–45
B10.2	G	T5	MTH 3-19a, MTH 4-18b, MTH 4-19a	N/A	**SYNCHRONISED SWIMMING** Transformations	46–47
B9.1, 9.2, 9.3	G	T1, T2	MTH 3-17a	G	**GYMNASTICS** Solving angle problems	48–49
B6.1; C4.4, 7.1	G	T1, T2	MNU 3-10a, MNU 4-10b	G	**PARALYMPIC ROAD CYCLING** Real-life graphs	50–51
A13.3, 13.4; B6.2	S	T2, T5	MTH 4-20a,b	F, G	**PENTATHLON** Averages and range	52–53
B3.6; C4.2, 4.4	N	T2, T5	MNU 3-07a, MNU 4-07a	F, G	**ENERGY CENTRE** Number skills 2	54–55

MATHS AND SCIENCE SERIES 2012

The London 2012 Olympic and Paralympic Games will be the largest sporting event ever staged in the UK. Without the maths skills of its organisers, engineers and architects, none of it would be possible.

The *Maths and Science Series 2012* gives you the chance to find out more about the events and venues of London 2012, whilst practising maths and science skills. The full range of free resources available in the series is listed in the table below.

TIPS FOR TEACHERS
CURRICULUM

To see how the contents of this book map onto the GCSE and SCQF curriculums, turn to page 8. Here you will find mappings to the most popular specifications in England, Scotland, Wales and Northern Ireland.

Print resources	Online resources www.mathsandscience2012.co.uk	Challenge 2012

The Activity Books will help bring London 2012 to life in the classroom. 15 copies of the Maths Activity Book and 15 copies of the Science Activity Book will be sent to every state-funded Secondary school in the UK.	The Maths and Science ActiveTeach can be accessed for free on our website. As well as having an electronic version of the book, the ActiveTeach contains great videos, and lots of helpful teaching resources.	The Maths and Science Challenge 2012 is a project-based competition open to all UK state-funded Secondary schools. It gives students the chance to imagine what a major sporting event might look like in their area.

Using your Maths Activity Book

The Maths Activity Book has been designed for Key Stage 4. It targets GCSE grades C and D, so it covers maths that all students need for their exams.

Bronze, Silver and Gold activities on each double-page spread offer stepped questions around the same maths topic. Bronze activities should take about 10 minutes to complete, and test basic skills and knowledge. Silver and Gold activities should take about 15–20 minutes to complete, testing problem-solving ability.

Mathematical topics are clearly labelled so you can make sure you're ready to tackle each section

Network infrastructure boxes highlight the maths and science skills Cisco engineers used to network the London 2012 Games

Straightforward Bronze activities are a great way to get started

Links to videos on the website

Silver activities are a bit more challenging, but still use maths skills familiar to students

Gold activities provide an opportunity for students to test the problem-solving skills they'll need in their exams

Stacks of facts about venues, events and athletes

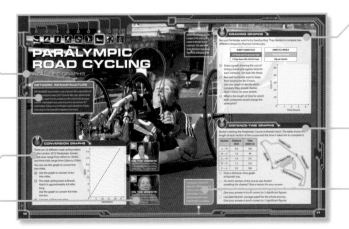

Using your Maths ActiveTeach

The Maths ActiveTeach is the e-book edition of your Maths Activity Book. As well as having an electronic version of the book, the ActiveTeach also contains high-impact videos. You can access the ActiveTeach online at www.mathsandscience2012.co.uk/activeteach. It's free and straightforward to use, with no registration or password needed.

You can also display the ActiveTeach on a classroom whiteboard. You can zoom into key areas of the book, and explore the video clips using direct links from the page.

Direct links to videos engage students and enrich lessons

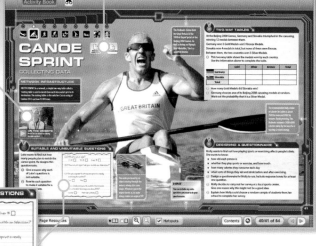

Zoom areas make it easy to focus on a specific activity

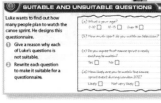

Maths and Science Challenge 2012

The Maths and Science Challenge 2012 gives students the chance to design a major sporting event in their area. Teams choose an event and a venue, then solve some of the problems facing the organisers of any London 2012 event. Every entry will include a short video, giving students a chance to explain their great ideas and brilliant maths and science skills.

Could the mountain biking be hosted in your area?

The best eight teams in the country will come to Cisco House, overlooking the Olympic Park in London, to battle it out for the top prizes – London 2012 tickets! In addition, winning teams will receive cash prizes for their STEM Club and London 2012 merchandise.

The competition is being run in association with STEMNET as STEM Challenge 10.

So get a team together and get planning!

MATHS AND SCIENCE SERIES 2012

Cisco

Official network infrastructure supporter of the London 2012 Olympic and Paralympic Games

The *Maths and Science Series 2012* has been proudly supported by Cisco, the official network infrastructure supporter of the London 2012 Olympic and Paralympic Games.

Cisco has provided the digital network infrastructure which will help enable pictures, video and results from every London 2012 event and venue to be shared with the rest of the world.

Cisco's network infrastructure for London 2012 will allow athletes, organisers, journalists and spectators to interconnect, access key London 2012 time applications, and connect to the internet at super-fast speeds, using either wired connections in over 100 London 2012 venues or wi-fi coverage throughout the venues and Olympic Park.

Cisco began life in 1984 in San Francisco, USA, when a married couple working at Stanford University designed a router which allowed computers made by different manufacturers to talk to each other. It took its name from the city where it was founded.

Now Cisco operates around the world and employs over 60 000 people. Since it began, the company has revolutionised the speeds at which digital data can be sent, has enabled millions of people to access the internet wirelessly, and has pioneered new technologies for video conferencing. Without Cisco's technologies, social networking, online gaming and downloading music and video wouldn't be possible.

Maths and science are at the heart of computing and networking, and the skills you practise in this book could one day help you design the next world-changing social network, or ground-breaking internet technology.

Cisco's 2 metre-tall CR-3 router forms part of the backbone of the internet. Using a 40-core low power QuantumFlow processor, this beast can transmit 322 terabits of data every second. That's enough bandwidth to stream 16 million high definition videos simultaneously!

Network infrastructure

Throughout this book we'll be showing you how Cisco's network infrastructure will play a crucial role in the smooth running of the London 2012 Games. You'll also learn about some of the maths involved in setting up and running a high-speed network. Just look for the network infrastructure fact boxes like this one.

NETWORK INFRASTRUCTURE

DID YOU KNOW? Cisco's network infrastructure at London 2012 is capable of transmitting over 10 GB of information each second. In the time it takes Usain Bolt to run the 100 m you could download the entire contents of Wikipedia. Twice.

www.mathsandscience2012.co.uk

Go online for the interactive editions of both the Maths and Science Activity Books, along with video clips and other features.

Out of the blocks

MATHS & SCIENCE SERIES 2012

CISCO
Official network infrastructure partner

2 5 2 DAYS TO GO

| Home | News | The Series | ActiveTeach | Challenge 2012 | Your A-Levels | Your Career | About Us |

Bring London 2012 to life in your classroom.

Your free Key Stage 4 resources inspired by the London 2012 Olympic and Paralympic Games.

Cisco, the official network infrastructure supporter of London 2012, is providing free maths and science resources to all state-funded Secondary Schools. Out of the Blocks gives you the chance to explore the events and venues of London 2012 whilst practising your maths and science skills.

Sign up to our email alerts to stay up-to-date with all the latest series and challenge news.

Watch Ellen MacArthur talk about her career transformation from sailor to campaigner.

NEWS HEADLINES

Sustainable Velodrome wins Better Public Building Award
If you're looking for some inspiration for your Challenge 2012 venue, the London...

Olympic Stadium track unveiled for the first time
Some of Britain's top athletes used the track in the Olympic Stadium for the first...

Maths and Science Challenge 2012

Click to enter!

low us on Twitter   Sign up to our email alerts to get involved   Like us on Facebook by clic

Follow   Like 104   You Tube

Help   Accessibility   Privacy Policy   Terms and Conditions   Contact Us

100m SPRINT

NUMBER SKILLS 1

NETWORK INFRASTRUCTURE

DID YOU KNOW? Cisco's network infrastructure at London 2012 is capable of transmitting over 10 GB of information each second. In the time it takes Usain Bolt to run the 100 m you could download the entire contents of Wikipedia. Twice.

FRACTIONS AND DECIMALS

The first sprinter to run the 100 m in less than 10 seconds at an Olympic Games was the USA's Jim Hines. At Mexico City 1968 he won Gold in 9.95 seconds.

1 An athlete leaves the starting blocks $\frac{1}{5}$ of a second after the starting gun is fired. Write $\frac{1}{5}$ as a decimal number.

2 a Write 9.95 as a mixed number.

  b By how much did Jim Hines break the 10-second barrier? Give your answer in seconds as a decimal number.

  c Write your answer to part **b** as a fraction in lowest terms.

3 Jim Hines' time was set with a tailwind of 1.6 m/s. This might have reduced his 100 m time by $\frac{3}{25}$ second. Use this value to estimate what Hines' 100 m time would have been with no wind.

MIXED NUMBERS

In the 4 × 100 m relay, four sprinters each run 100 m. In legs 2, 3 and 4 the sprinters can start with a run-up so their 100 m times are quicker.

This table shows the times of each leg in a 4 × 100 m relay race.

	Leg 1 (s)	Leg 2 (s)	Leg 3 (s)	Leg 4 (s)
Team 1	9.81	9.30	8.94	9.22
Team 2	10.02	$9\frac{1}{10}$	$8\frac{4}{5}$	$9\frac{1}{4}$
Team 3	9.85	$8\frac{17}{20}$	$9\frac{1}{2}$	9.39

1 Write down
  a the fastest leg run in the race
  b the slowest leg run in the race.

2 Which team won the relay race? Show all of your working.

Usain Bolt won Gold Medals in the 100 m and the 200 m at the Beijing 2008 Games, setting new world records in both events. Will he do it again at London 2012?

SOLVING FRACTION PROBLEMS

After Usain Bolt's 100 m triumph at Beijing 2008, his father revealed his Gold Medal-winning diet secret: yams. Bolt even has custom-made trainers designed to be the same colour as the high-energy root vegetable!

1. A sprinter eats $\frac{3}{8}$ kg of yams each day.
   How many kilograms of yams should he bring to London to see him through the 15 days of the 2012 Games?

2. In a typical meal for an athlete:
   - $\frac{3}{5}$ is protein
   - $\frac{1}{10}$ is fat
   - the rest is carbohydrate.

   An athlete's lunch contains 225 g of carbohydrate.

   How much protein is there in this meal?

3. A bowl of spicy yam soup contains 210 calories.
   $\frac{2}{7}$ of these calories come from fat.
   15% of the fat calories are from saturated fat.
   Work out the number of calories from unsaturated fat in a bowl of spicy yam soup.

PARALYMPIC HEROES

Double amputee Oscar Pistorius won 3 Gold Medals at Beijing 2008. His carbon fibre artificial limbs have earned him the nickname 'Blade Runner'.

PARALYMPIC ARCHERY

CIRCLES

NETWORK INFRASTRUCTURE

DID YOU KNOW? Computer engineers often test processor speeds by calculating the value of π to lots of decimal places. The 8-core processors in Cisco's network infrastructure firewalls could calculate π to 50 000 decimal places in the time it takes an arrow to travel from the bow to the target.

In the Paralympic Games, archers have to aim at a target 70 m away. Half a degree in either direction could be the difference between a bullseye and missing the target completely.

CIRCUMFERENCE

The diagram shows the archery target that will be used at London 2012.
The target is made from concentric circles in five different colours.

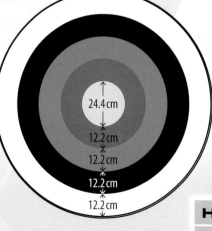

24.4 cm
12.2 cm
12.2 cm
12.2 cm
12.2 cm

1 An archer lands an arrow 45 cm from the centre of the target. Which colour does the arrow land in?

2 Work out the circumference of the yellow circle at the centre of the target. Give your answer to 3 significant figures.

3 a Work out the diameter of the whole target.

   b What is the circumference of the whole target? Give your answer to 3 significant figures.

HINT

Concentric circles all have the same centre.

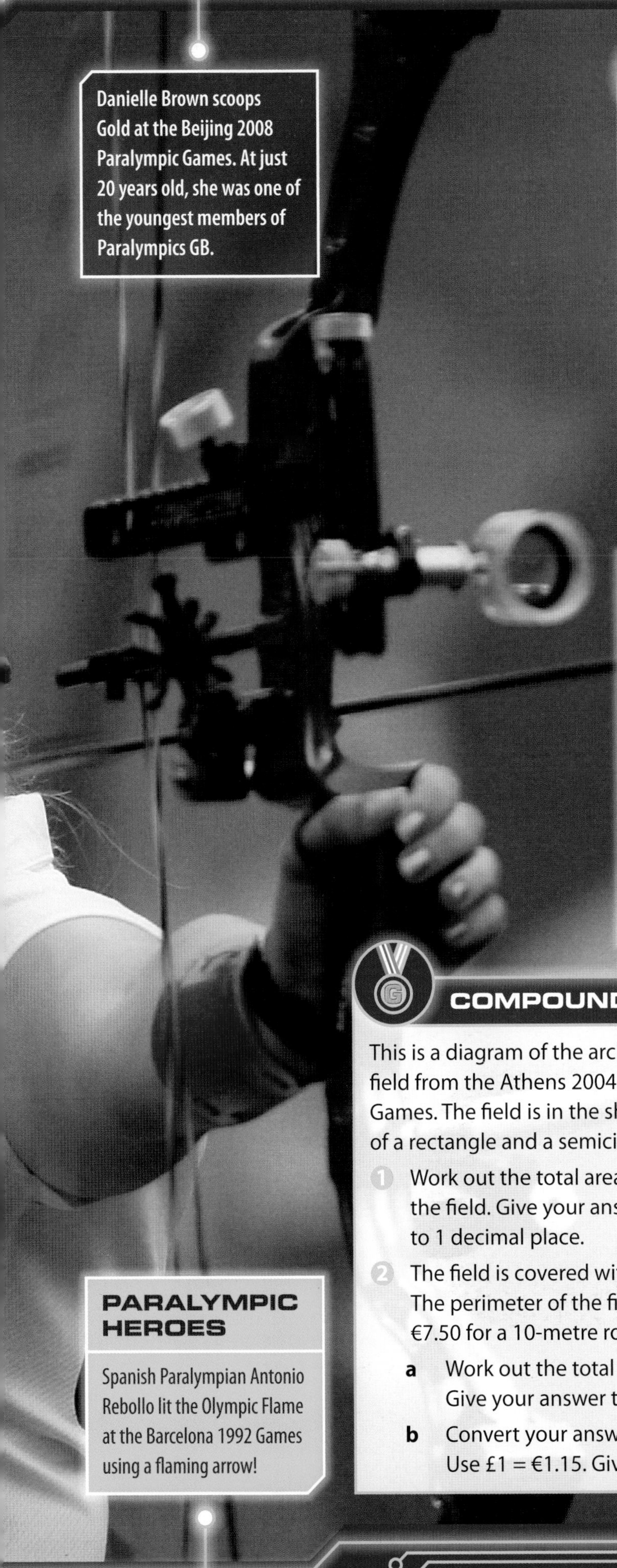

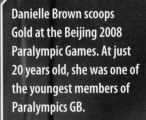

Danielle Brown scoops Gold at the Beijing 2008 Paralympic Games. At just 20 years old, she was one of the youngest members of Paralympics GB.

AREA OF A CIRCLE

Look at the archery target on the opposite page.

1. Work out the area of the yellow circle at the centre of the target.
   Give your answer to 3 significant figures.

2. Carla says that the blue area on the target is more than twice as large as the red area.
   Is Carla correct? Show all of your working.

3. Carla draws a new practice target. She wants her practice target to be a solid circle with the same area as the black ring on the London 2012 target. Work out the radius of Carla's practice target, correct to 3 significant figures.

At the Athens 2004 Games the archery competition took place on the site of an ancient Greek stadium.

COMPOUND SHAPES

This is a diagram of the archery field from the Athens 2004 Games. The field is in the shape of a rectangle and a semicircle.

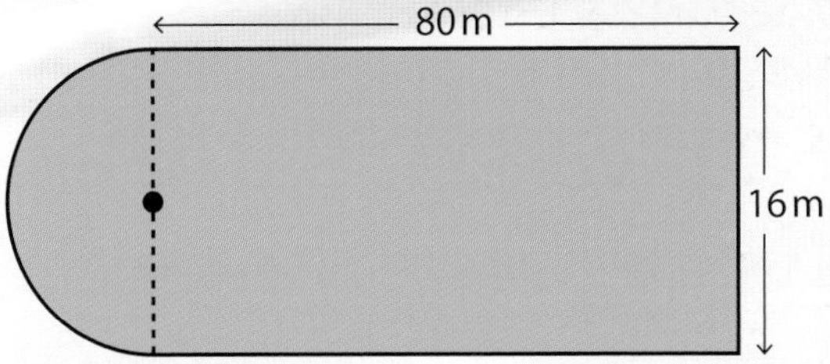

1. Work out the total area of the field. Give your answer to 1 decimal place.

2. The field is covered with artificial turf. The turf costs €15 per square metre. The perimeter of the field is marked with safety tape. Safety tape costs €7.50 for a 10-metre roll.

   a. Work out the total cost of the artificial turf and safety tape. Give your answer to the nearest euro.

   b. Convert your answer to part **a** into pounds.
      Use £1 = €1.15. Give your answer to the nearest pound.

Diagram labels: 80 m, 16 m

PARALYMPIC HEROES

Spanish Paralympian Antonio Rebollo lit the Olympic Flame at the Barcelona 1992 Games using a flaming arrow!

WATER POLO

STRAIGHT-LINE GRAPHS

NETWORK INFRASTRUCTURE

DID YOU KNOW? Every event at London 2012 will be filmed in HD. The relationship between the extra data traffic generated by HD video and the amount of power needed by the processors (known as ASICs) in Cisco's network infrastructure can be described using a straight-line graph.

NAMING LINES

This is an architect's diagram of the Water Polo Arena. The red lines show some of the structural features and sightlines.

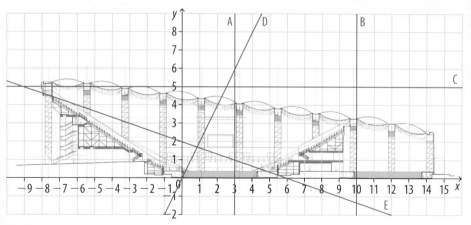

1. Write down the equations of lines A, B and C.

2. **a** Work out the gradient of line D.

   b Write down the equation of line D in the form $y = mx$.

3. The gradient of line E is $-\frac{1}{3}$. Write down the equation of line E in the form $y = mx + c$.

The umpires' desk is on one side of the pool. Architects designed the Water Polo Arena to have more seats on the other side, to give members of the public the best possible view of the action.

STRAIGHT-LINE GRAPHS

The diagram below shows part of the lighting plan for the Water Polo Arena. The area each light covers is defined by two equations.

Light	Coordinates	Equations of beam limits	
A	$(-2, 5)$	$y = -x + 3$	$y = -\frac{1}{2}x + 4$
B	$(1, 5)$	$y = 2x + 3$	$x = 1$
C	$(7, 3)$	$2y - x + 1 = 0$	$y = x - 4$

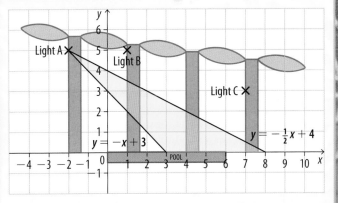

The beam limits for light A have been drawn.

1 **a** Draw a coordinate grid from −1 to 6 in the vertical direction and from −4 to 10 in the horizontal direction. Mark the positions of the lights and the pool on your coordinate grid.

b Draw the beams for lights B and C. You can use tables of values to help you. Label each line with its equation.

2 Will the three lights cover the whole of the pool?

MIDPOINTS OF LINE SEGMENTS

Water polo players often position themselves half way between two other players to block a pass. The point half way between two points A and B on a coordinate grid is called the midpoint of the line segment AB.

1 This table shows the positions of three pairs of players. For each pair of players, find the midpoint to work out the best position to block a pass.

2 Ahmed is blocking a pass between Ben and Karl. He positions himself at (−2, 1), half way between the two players. Karl is at (3, 5). Work out Ben's coordinates.

	First player	Second player
a	(0, 2)	(6, 4)
b	(−1, 5)	(3, 1)
c	(2, 7)	(−5, −6)

HINT

If A has coordinates (x_1, y_1) and B has coordinates (x_2, y_2) the coordinates of the midpoint are $\left(\dfrac{x_1 + x_2}{2}, \dfrac{y_1 + y_2}{2} \right)$

DIVING
FORMULAE

NETWORK INFRASTRUCTURE

DID YOU KNOW? In damp and wet environments, Cisco will protect its wireless network access points using waterproof enclosures. These enclosures are tested to withstand jets of water with a flow rate of 100 litres per minute for up to 3 minutes.

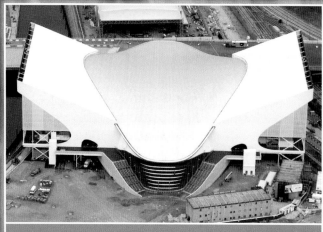

The 'wings' of the Aquatics Centre will allow it to hold 17 500 spectators during London 2012. After the 2012 Games the wings will be removed, leaving a world-class 2500-seater facility.

USING FORMULAE

Ashley wants to do a forward somersault dive. She can add twists to the dive to increase its difficulty. She uses this formula to work out the difficulty of her dive:

$$D = 1.5 + 0.4 \times T$$

D is the difficulty of the dive and T is the number of twists.

1. Work out the difficulty of this dive if Ashley includes half a twist.
2. Rearrange Ashley's formula to make T the subject.
3. Ashley eventually decides on a dive with a difficulty rating of 2.7. How many twists does Ashley include in her dive?

The Aquatics Centre for London 2012 will have diving platforms at heights of 3 m, 5 m, 7.5 m and 10 m.

FOLLOWING A RULE

There are seven judges in the diving event.
Each judge gives a 'raw' score out of 10.

You can use these steps to work out the final score for each dive.

> Write the 7 'raw' scores in order of size.

> Cross off the highest and lowest scores.

> Work out the mean of the remaining scores.

> Multiply this value by $\frac{3}{5}$.

> Multiply your answer by the difficulty rating.

This table shows the judges' raw scores for dives by two different competitors.

	Difficulty rating	Judges' raw scores						
		1	2	3	4	5	6	7
Rhys	3.2	9.0	9.5	9.0	8.5	7.5	8.5	8.0
Adam	3.5	8.5	7.0	7.5	8.5	8.0	7.5	9.0

Who had the higher final score?
Show all of your working.

REARRANGING FORMULAE

You can use this formula to estimate the time it takes a diver to hit the water:

$$t = \sqrt{\frac{h}{5}}$$

t is the time in seconds and h is the height in metres.

① Ella dives off the 3 m diving platform. Use the formula to estimate the time she takes to hit the water. Give your answer to 3 significant figures.

② At the same time, Sajid dives off the 7.5 m platform. How much later does he hit the water than Ella? Give your answer to 3 significant figures.

③ Ella tries a second dive. It takes her 1 second to hit the water.

  a Rearrange the formula to make h the subject.

  b Which diving platform did Ella use?

HINT

Start by squaring both sides of the formula.

CYCLING
REPRESENTING DATA

Team GB sets a new world record on its way to winning Gold in the Men's Team Pursuit at the Beijing 2008 Games. The cyclists are following each other with a gap of just $\frac{1}{100}$ of a second.

NETWORK INFRASTRUCTURE

DID YOU KNOW? With no opportunity for second chances, week-long 'technical rehearsals' will make sure everything is working as planned. Cisco Network Management software collects data about how each component performs, which can be represented in graphs and charts. During the 2012 Games, this software can send live updates to Cisco engineers via text message.

ON THE WEBSITE
Watch videos showing the building of the Velodrome and the VeloPark it will become after London 2012.

The Velodrome was one of the first venues to be completed. It has been nicknamed 'the Pringle' because of the shape of its roof.

STEM-AND-LEAF DIAGRAMS

In a pursuit race, cyclists start on opposite sides of the track and try to overtake each other. Here are the qualifying times in seconds from the Women's Individual Pursuit at Beijing 2008.

| 221 | 237 | 215 | 208 | 224 | 212 | 220 | 218 | 226 | 209 | 216 | 214 | 221 |

1. Show this information in an ordered stem-and-leaf diagram.
2. Work out the range of this data.
3. What was the median time for this qualifying round?

This was Rebecca Romero's time. She went on to win a Gold Medal for Great Britain.

OLYMPIC HEROES

Chris Hoy won a hat-trick of Gold Medals at Beijing 2008. He advised the architects on the construction of the London 2012 Velodrome.

SCATTER DIAGRAMS

Imran is investigating the effect of air temperature on cyclists' speeds. He times a cyclist over 4 km on six different practice rides at different temperatures. This table shows his results.

Temperature (°C)	28	20	32	26	18	23
Time (seconds)	282	286	280	284	293	288

❶ Draw a scatter diagram for Imran's data. Use axes like these.

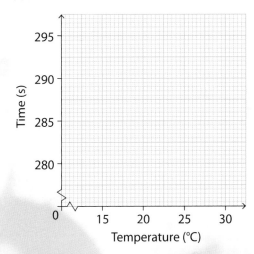

❷ Draw a line of best fit on your scatter diagram.

❸ Imran says that if the temperature inside the Velodrome was 50 °C then the cyclist would complete the race in under 270 seconds. Do you agree with Imran's statement? Explain your answer.

FREQUENCY POLYGONS

Team GB used a revolutionary low-drag skinsuit at the Beijing 2008 Games. This table shows how 20 cyclists performed in a time trial with and without the hi-tech suit.

Time, t (s)	Frequency without skinsuit	Frequency with skinsuit
$260 < t \leqslant 270$	0	4
$270 < t \leqslant 280$	6	10
$280 < t \leqslant 290$	12	5
$290 < t \leqslant 300$	2	1

❶ Draw frequency polygons for both sets of data on the same axes.

❷ Use your frequency polygons to compare the performance of the cyclists with and without the skinsuit. Give reasons for your answers.

The low-drag 'skinsuits' used by Team GB at Beijing 2008 were so top-secret that they were shredded after the Games so nobody could steal the technology.

SAILING
MAPS AND BEARINGS

OLYMPIC HEROES

Ben Ainslie won Silver at Atlanta 1996, and then went on to win Gold at Sydney 2000, Athens 2004 and Beijing 2008. He has also been selected to represent Great Britain at London 2012.

BEARINGS AND DISTANCES 1

1 The sailing venue for the 2012 Games is Weymouth and Portland, 125 miles from the Olympic Park. This map shows all the London 2012 venues that are outside London.

   a Measure the bearing of London from Weymouth and Portland.

   b How far is it in a straight line from Old Trafford to Hampden Park?

   c Write down the bearing and distance of the Millennium Stadium from St James' Park.

2 A Finn Class racing yacht leaves the harbour in Weymouth and Portland and travels in a straight line on a bearing of 120°. Work out the bearing of its return journey.

N

Scale:
1 cm = 100 miles

Hampden Park

St James' Park

Old Trafford

City of Coventry Stadium

Lee Valley White Water Centre

Eton Dorney

Hadleigh Farm

Millennium Stadium

London

Brands Hatch

Weymouth and Portland

BEARINGS AND DISTANCES 2

This map shows the Olympic and Paralympic Sailing competition area at Weymouth and Portland.

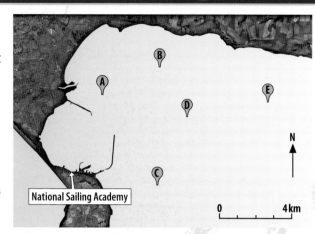

National Sailing Academy

0   4 km

1 Nick needs to place a buoy at each of the five locations marked with a letter. Plan a route his speedboat can take to visit all five locations. He can visit the five locations in any order. Your route should start and end at the National Sailing Academy.

For each leg of Nick's journey write down the bearing and the distance travelled. Record your route in a table like this one.

From	To	Bearing	Distance
Academy	B	041°	7.4 km
B			

2 Work out the total length of your route. Can you find a route which is less than 35 km long?

HINT

Make sure you avoid the harbour walls on your way in and out of the National Sailing Academy.

SOLVING PROBLEMS WITH SCALE DRAWINGS

Yacht A is competing in an Olympic Sailing race.

Yacht B is 8.6 km due east of Yacht A.

Yacht C is 10 km from Yacht A on a bearing of 215°.

1 Use a scale drawing to work out the distance between Yacht B and Yacht C.

Yacht D is due south of Yacht B.

Yacht D is on a bearing of 080° from Yacht C.

2 Mark the position of Yacht D on your scale drawing.

3 Measure the bearing and distance of Yacht A from Yacht D.

HINT

Use a scale of 1 cm = 2 km

DECATHLON
EQUATIONS

NETWORK INFRASTRUCTURE

DID YOU KNOW? High Density (spotlight) wi-fi access points mean that everyone in the Olympic Stadium can check up on the latest London 2012 results! Cisco network infrastructure engineers use complex sets of equations (known as algorithms) to tune the power of each hotspot, making sure they don't interfere with each other.

OLYMPIC HEROES

Female athletes compete in the seven-event Heptathlon. Great Britain's Denise Lewis won a Heptathlon Gold Medal at the Sydney 2000 Games, struggling through injury to finish just a few points ahead of her nearest rival.

SOLVING EQUATIONS

Solve these equations to find key London 2012 facts and figures.

1 The number of world records Daley Thompson held:

$$2(n + 3) = 14$$

2 The height in metres a decathlete needs to clear to score 1000 points in the high jump event:

$$3h - 10 = 1 - 2h$$

3 The price in pounds of a top-price ticket to the first day of the Decathlon:

$$3(p - 50) = 2p$$

4 The time in minutes it will take the Javelin high-speed rail link to travel between St Pancras Station and the Olympic Park in Stratford:

$$3(m + 1) - 5(m - 3) = 4$$

WRITING YOUR OWN EQUATIONS

The long jump is one of the 10 events which make up the Olympic Decathlon.

1 This decathlete is taking off for the long jump.

   a Write down an equation in terms of angle x.

   b Solve your equation to work out the angle of take-off.

2 This long jump pit is a rectangle $\frac{1}{2}(n + 1)$ m wide and $(2n - 1)$ m long.

   The perimeter of the long jump pit is 24 m.

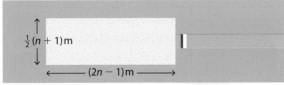

Work out the area of the long jump pit.

OLYMPIC HEROES

British decathlete Daley Thompson won Olympic Gold Medals in 1980 and 1984.

TRIAL AND IMPROVEMENT

In the shot put event, decathletes have to throw a 7.25 kg metal ball as far as possible. At the Beijing 2008 Games, US Gold Medallist Bryan Clay threw the shot put 16.27 m.

You can use this equation to estimate the speed of the shot put when it left his hand.
x is the speed in m/s.

$$x^2 + x\sqrt{4x^2 + 64} = 500$$

Use trial and improvement to solve this equation. Give your value of x correct to 1 decimal place. Use a table like this to show your working.

x	$x^2 + x\sqrt{4x^2 + 64}$	Too high or too low	Comment
10	315.406…	Too low	$x > 10$

ROWING

SPEED AND COMPOUND MEASURES

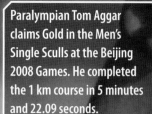
NETWORK INFRASTRUCTURE

DID YOU KNOW? Cisco's high-speed network infrastructure can transmit signals 45 km from the rowing venue at Eton Dorney back to the Olympic Park in less than 0.005 seconds. That's an average signal speed of 9 million m/s.

SPEED, DISTANCE AND TIME

This table shows Team GB's medal-winning results from the Beijing 2008 Games. All these events took place over a 2000 m course.

Event	Medal won	Time (s)	Average speed (m/s)
Men's Lightweight Double Sculls	Gold	371	5.39
Men's Coxless Four	Gold	367	
Women's Quadruple Sculls	Silver		5.30
Men's Coxed Eight	Silver		6.15
Women's Double Sculls	Bronze	428	
Men's Double Sculls	Bronze		5.14

Copy and complete the table, working out the missing values.
Give your answers correct to 3 significant figures.

HINT

Use the formula triangle for speed to help you.

The discovery of a buried Anglo-Saxon woman raised eyebrows when the Eton Dorney rowing centre was under construction. Archaeologists suggested that her isolated location could indicate that she had been accused of witchcraft!

COMPOUND MEASURES

Rowers have to decide how many strokes they take each minute.
More strokes mean a faster speed, but they'll get tired more quickly.

1. In a practice row, Nisha takes 209 strokes in 5 minutes and 30 seconds.
   a. Calculate her stroke rate in strokes per minute.
   b. How many more strokes would she take if she continued rowing at this rate for another 30 seconds?

2. In a second row Nisha increases her stroke rate to 40 strokes per minute. How long does it take her to take 250 strokes? Give your answer in minutes and seconds.

HINT
Remember there are 60 seconds in 1 minute, so 5 minutes and 30 seconds is the same as $5\frac{30}{60}$ or $5\frac{1}{2}$ minutes.

PROBLEM SOLVING

In Olympic and Paralympic Rowing, split times are measured every 500 m.

Here are some split times for a 2000 m race at Eton Dorney. The table shows the time in seconds when the crews passed each timing point.

	Start	A	B	C	Finish
Red crew	0	104	199	291	380
Blue crew	0	90	195	292	395

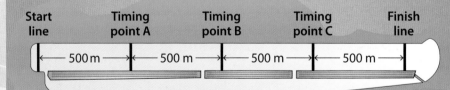

1. a. Work out the average speed of the red crew between the start line and timing point A. Give your answer in m/s to 1 decimal place.
   b. Convert your answer to part **a** into km/h.

2. How far behind was the blue crew when the red crew crossed the finish line? You can assume that the blue crew travelled at a constant speed between timing point C and the finish line.

3. The green crew completed the course at an average speed of 19 km/h. Did they win the race? Show all of your working.

MEDIA CENTRE

RATIO AND PROPORTION

NETWORK INFRASTRUCTURE

DID YOU KNOW? More than 16 000 journalists will use Cisco's network infrastructure to take advantage of a 40 Gb internet connection. This is 3000 times as much bandwidth as an average home broadband connection, so stories, pictures and videos can be uploaded and downloaded in record time.

WORKING WITH RATIOS

The Media Centre is divided into the Main Press Centre (MPC), the International Broadcast Centre (IBC) and the catering village.

International Broadcast Centre (IBC)

Main Press Centre (MPC)

Catering village

The floor areas of the MPC and the catering village are in the ratio 5 : 3.

The floor areas of the MPC and the IBC are in the ratio 2 : 5.

In the IBC, the ratio of studio space to office space is 23 : 7.

1 The floor area of the catering village is 18 000 m². Work out the floor area of the MPC.

2 Work out the floor area of the IBC.

3 Calculate the floor area of the IBC which is used as office space.

During London 2012 the Media Centre will be buzzing with activity 24 hours a day. A live link-up with a midday news programme in Sydney would have to take place at 3 am London time!

FRACTIONS AND RATIOS

Spectators at the London 2012 Games will come from all over the world. Spectators from London, the rest of the UK, and overseas are expected to be in the ratio 5 : 9 : 6.

$\frac{5}{6}$ of the overseas spectators are expected to come from European countries.

1 What fraction of the total number of spectators are expected to come

   a   from London

   b   from countries outside Europe?

2 750 000 spectators are expected to come from European countries other than the UK. Estimate the number of UK spectators from outside London. Show all of your working.

PROPORTION

Individual journalists will be able to book internet bandwidth at certain times to upload and download photos and video. Two journalists are downloading video files. The diagrams show their progress.

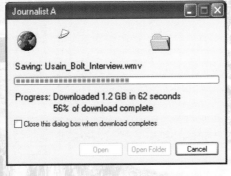

1 Work out which journalist has the faster internet connection. Show all of your working.

2 Which file is larger? Give a reason for your answer.

3 How long would it take

   a   journalist A to download a 790 MB file

   b   journalist B to download a 4.3 GB file?

HINT

There are 1000 MB in 1 GB.

DESIGNING A MAJOR SPORTING EVENT

1 LOCATION

NETWORK INFRASTRUCTURE

DID YOU KNOW? As well as providing the network infrastructure for every London 2012 venue, Cisco has linked up transport hubs, training grounds and ticketing booths. By using existing telephone exchanges and wires, Cisco engineers are able to network venues like the Lee Valley White Water Centre more efficiently.

At London 2012 the canoe slalom event will take place at the newly built Lee Valley White Water Centre. On the next six pages you will learn about some of the challenges of planning this major sporting event.

White Water Centre is the first of new London 2012 venues to be completed

November 2009 and construction is underway...

... and one year later the water is flowing.

The Lee Valley White Water Centre was opened in Spring 2011. It is 30 km north of the Olympic Park, and is part of the Lee Valley Regional Park which stretches 26 miles along the banks of the River Lee. Park visitors can take advantage of cycle and walking trails, a golf course and an athletics centre.

CHALLENGE 2012

PLAN AN EVENT NEAR *YOUR* SCHOOL

Could you design a major sporting event in your area? The Maths and Science Challenge 2012 gives you an opportunity to do just that.

Choose a sport and a venue, then use your maths and science skills to plan your event. Tackle some of the problems faced by London 2012 organisers and create a video telling us why your event is so great. You could be in with a chance of winning Challenge 2012! So get a team together, find a willing teacher, and get planning.

For more information visit www.mathsandscience2012.co.uk/challenge2012

ON THE WEBSITE
Watch some of Britain's medal hopes welcome you to Challenge 2012.

Up to 60 000 spectators are expected to watch the canoe slalom event at the Lee Valley White Water Centre. Temporary stands will mean they all have a great view.

CHALLENGE 2012

CHOOSING A SPORT

Choosing a popular sport or one where Team GB have a good chance of winning medals will help you ensure a sell-out crowd.

Canoeing becomes fastest growing water sport in UK

With 1.2 million participants in 2010, canoeing has surged in popularity in recent years.

At Beijing 2008, Great Britain's David Florence won a Silver Medal in the canoe slalom. It's a fast and exciting sport, which is one of the reasons why tickets to the canoe slalom sessions at London 2012 were so popular.

In the London 2012 canoe slalom, 82 athletes will compete for four Gold Medals. Competitors must negotiate a course of up to 25 coloured gates. Touching a gate means a 2-second penalty. Missing a gate completely results in an unrecoverable 50-second penalty.

David Florence claims Silver at Beijing 2008

Great public transport links help visitors take greener option

The Lee Valley White Water Centre is a 10-minute walk from Waltham Cross train station or a 20-minute walk from Cheshunt train station. During London 2012, spectators with tickets to the canoe slalom will receive a Games Travelcard. This will entitle them to free travel on London public transport on the day of the event, and on National Rail services between London and the White Water Centre.

Maths Skills

1. Look at the information in the newspaper article above. The population of the UK is 62 million. What percentage of the UK population participates in canoeing? Give your answer to 1 decimal place.

2. Look at the information above about transport links to the White Water Centre. Here is part of a train timetable.

Stratford DLR ⊖ .... d		0733			0803		0820				0858	
Seven Sisters ⊖ .... d												
Tottenham Hale ⊖ .... d	0740	0743	0753	0810	0813	0825	0829	0840	0855	0910	0914	0925
Northumberland Park .... d		0745			0815		0832				0916	
Angel Road .... d		0747			0817		0834				0918	
Ponders End .... d			0759			0829			0859			0929
Brimsdown .... d			0802			0832			0902			0932
Enfield Lock .... d		0752	0804		0822	0834	0839		0904		0923	0934
Waltham Cross 🚌 .... d			0807			0837			0907			0937
Cheshunt 🚌 .... d	0748	0756	0809	0818	0826	0839	0842	0848	0909	0918	0927	0939
Broxbourne 🚌 .... a	0752	0800	0814	0822	0830	0844	0847	0852	0914	0922	0931	0944

Shilpa is travelling from Stratford to the White Water Centre.
She needs to arrive by 9am.

a. Which train should Shilpa take?

b. Shilpa says that she will arrive at the White Water Centre earlier if she changes at Tottenham Hale and travels to Waltham Cross.
Is Shilpa correct? Show your working.

DESIGNING A MAJOR SPORTING EVENT

2 VENUE

Could you handle the Olympic Course?

The Lee Valley White Water Centre has two different courses, which are both open to the public. The Olympic Course is 300 m long and drops 5.5 m. The Legacy Loop is a less challenging intermediate course, which is 160 m long with a descent of 1.6 m.

The white water is created using a system of pumps and obstacles. The obstacles can be moved around to change the features of the course.

Both courses feature conveyor belts to carry canoes up to the start.

CHALLENGE 2012

DRAWING A PLAN

A plan of your venue can show its key features.

Olympic Course

Car park

Facilities building

Conveyor belts

Lake

Legacy Loop

Viewing areas

ON THE WEBSITE
Watch Colin Naish from the Olympic Delivery Authority talk about the canoe slalom course.

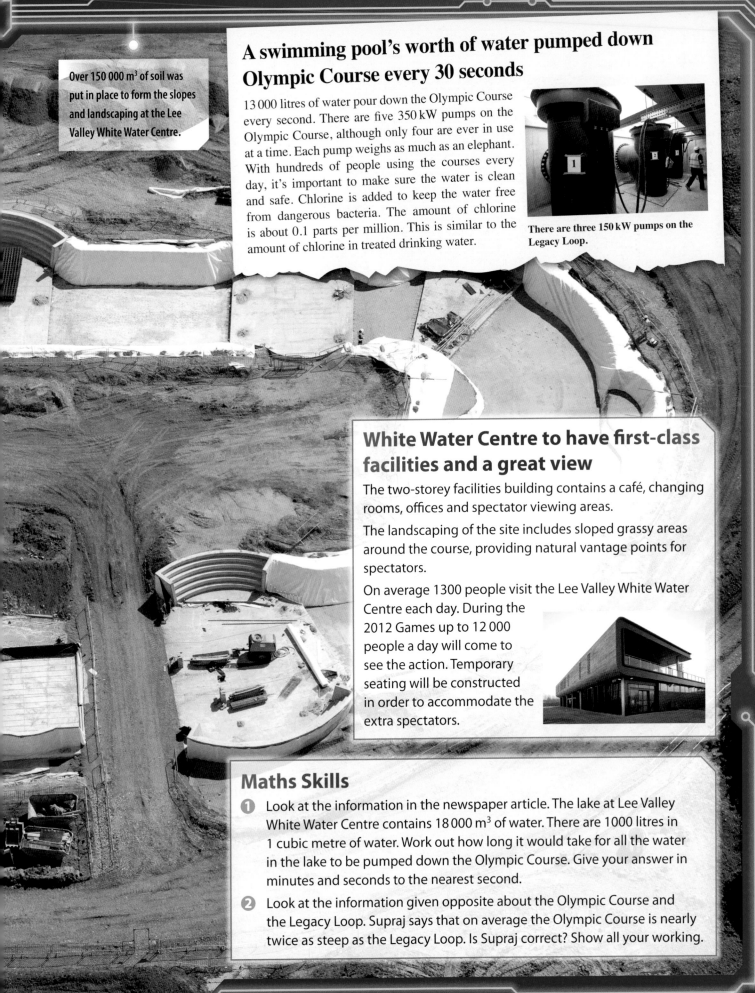

Over 150 000 m³ of soil was put in place to form the slopes and landscaping at the Lee Valley White Water Centre.

A swimming pool's worth of water pumped down Olympic Course every 30 seconds

13 000 litres of water pour down the Olympic Course every second. There are five 350 kW pumps on the Olympic Course, although only four are ever in use at a time. Each pump weighs as much as an elephant. With hundreds of people using the courses every day, it's important to make sure the water is clean and safe. Chlorine is added to keep the water free from dangerous bacteria. The amount of chlorine is about 0.1 parts per million. This is similar to the amount of chlorine in treated drinking water.

There are three 150 kW pumps on the Legacy Loop.

White Water Centre to have first-class facilities and a great view

The two-storey facilities building contains a café, changing rooms, offices and spectator viewing areas.

The landscaping of the site includes sloped grassy areas around the course, providing natural vantage points for spectators.

On average 1300 people visit the Lee Valley White Water Centre each day. During the 2012 Games up to 12 000 people a day will come to see the action. Temporary seating will be constructed in order to accommodate the extra spectators.

Maths Skills

1. Look at the information in the newspaper article. The lake at Lee Valley White Water Centre contains 18 000 m³ of water. There are 1000 litres in 1 cubic metre of water. Work out how long it would take for all the water in the lake to be pumped down the Olympic Course. Give your answer in minutes and seconds to the nearest second.

2. Look at the information given opposite about the Olympic Course and the Legacy Loop. Supraj says that on average the Olympic Course is nearly twice as steep as the Legacy Loop. Is Supraj correct? Show all your working.

NETWORK INFRASTRUCTURE

DID YOU KNOW? Cisco plans to set up 50 new Networking Academies in the London 2012 host boroughs. Through online courses, these programmes will train local people for highly-skilled jobs in ICT.

Birds, bats and biodiversity

Before building the White Water Centre a habitat management plan was created, showing how the impact of the centre on wildlife and the natural environment could be minimised.

A Gadwall duck

- 22 species of nesting bird were recorded in the area. Any removal of trees and plants was carried out before the birds began building their nests at the start of March.

- Bats do not like crossing well-lit areas to find food. During construction, lighting was directed away from the woodland edge and waterways, and 15 bat feeding boxes were installed.

- 1% of the world's population of the Gadwall duck and 1.5% of the world's population of the Shoveler duck spend their winter in the Lee Valley Regional Park. Buffer zones were created between the site and animal habitats in order to protect these water birds.

CHALLENGE 2012

DESIGNING FOR SUSTAINABILITY

Will your event be environmentally friendly? Using materials from sustainable sources for construction, and encouraging spectators and athletes to recycle are just two ways to minimise any negative impact on the local area.

White Water Centre will have something for everyone before and after the 2012 Games

The Lee Valley White Water Centre has been open to the public since Spring 2011. Thousands of people have already enjoyed the centre, and thousands more will continue to use it after the 2012 Games. In 2015 it will host the Canoe Slalom World Championships.

The area surrounding the White Water Centre is one of the most deprived in Hertfordshire. As well as creating 50 new jobs, the presence of a major leisure attraction benefits local businesses. Visitors use shops, restaurants and accommodation. In December 2009, a canoe and kayak shop opened opposite the site of the centre.

The White Water Centre has a full-time Youth and Schools programme, which works with local schools on a range of projects.

Footpaths around the Olympic Course will be open to the public after the 2012 Games.

Students can practise orienteering on the site, learn about leisure and tourism management, or explore the varied wildlife in the area. In June 2011 the centre hosted the White Water Schools Festival, with students from 126 schools rafting on the Olympic Course.

As well as canoeing, visitors to the Lee Valley White Water Centre can also experience white water rafting. This means a much wider range of people can make use of the centre after the 2012 Games.

CHALLENGE 2012

TRANSFORMING A COMMUNITY

Hosting a major sporting event can change an area or community dramatically. It's your responsibility to make sure that your event has a positive impact on your local area. Will the venue be used by the public after the event? Will it host other national or international competitions? What are the benefits to the local community? Can you plan activities which will involve students from local schools?

Maths Skills

① Charlie is designing a questionnaire to help him decide how popular canoeing is amongst students in his school.

a He writes this question:

> Canoeing is a brilliant sport to watch on TV isn't it?
>
> Yes ☐   No ☐

Charlie's question is unsuitable. Explain why.

b Rewrite Charlie's question to make it suitable.

c Charlie wants to know how many times each student participates in water sports each year. Write a suitable question for Charlie to use. Include response boxes with your question.

② Amy carried out a survey of 50 people who used the White Water Centre on one day last year. They had all come either to canoe, to raft or to watch.

- 31 of the people were female.
- Of the 8 people who had come to canoe, 6 were male.
- In total, 13 people were rafting.
- 9 male visitors were just watching.

a Draw a two-way table to represent this information.

b How many female visitors had come to watch?

BEACH VOLLEYBALL

AREA AND VOLUME

NETWORK INFRASTRUCTURE

DID YOU KNOW? Cisco will install around 300 m³ of network infrastructure equipment to make sure the London 2012 Games technology runs smoothly. Stacked on top of each other, the network switches would reach a height of over 230 m. That's the same as the London Eye and the Big Ben clock tower combined.

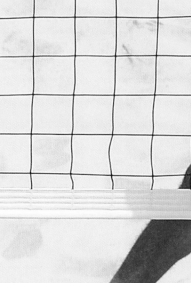

SHAPES MADE FROM RECTANGLES

The diagram shows the area of sand on each beach volleyball court. The playing area is shaded yellow. There is a 6 m wide strip of sand around the playing area. Green tape marks the edge of the sand.

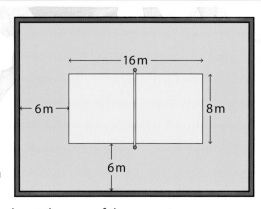

16 m

6 m

8 m

6 m

❶ What is the area of the whole rectangle of sand?

❷ Work out the area of sand which is not part of the playing area.

❸ The green tape is 15 cm wide. Work out the area of the green tape. Give your answer in m² to 1 decimal place.

AREAS OF COMPOUND SHAPES

Brea is designing a sports bag for the British beach volleyball team. The diagram shows the end panel of her bag.

Brea wants to include a logo on the bag. Olympic Regulations say that the logo must take up no more than 10% of the surface area of the panel.

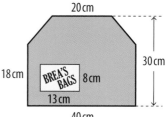

1 Work out the area of the whole end panel.

2 Does Brea's design satisfy the Olympic Regulations? Show all of your working.

The beach volleyball will take place on Horse Guards Parade in central London, just 100 m away from 10 Downing Street.

In beach volleyball a one-handed block is called a 'Kong'. The name comes from the way King Kong swatted biplanes whilst climbing the Empire State Building!

VOLUME AND DENSITY

The London 2012 beach volleyball venue has five courts with the dimensions shown on the opposite page. Each court is filled with sand to a depth of 50 cm. Underneath the sand is a 20 cm layer of gravel.

The density of sand is 1600 kg/m³.

The density of gravel is 1700 kg/m³.

Estimate the total mass of sand and gravel used in the construction of the five beach volleyball courts. Give your answer to 3 significant figures and show all your working.

CANOE SPRINT

COLLECTING DATA

NETWORK INFRASTRUCTURE

DID YOU KNOW? In a network, a simple two-way table called a 'routing table' is used to decide how each data packet gets to its destination. The routing tables in the switches Cisco is using at London 2012 can have 12 000 rows.

ON THE WEBSITE
Watch Tim talk about his training schedule and diet.

SUITABLE AND UNSUITABLE QUESTIONS

Luke wants to find out how many people plan to watch the canoe sprint. He designs this questionnaire.

1. Give a reason why each of Luke's questions is not suitable.

2. Rewrite each question to make it suitable for a questionnaire.

(a) What is your age?

   0-10 ☐   10-15 ☐   Over 18 ☐

(b) How much sport do you watch on television?

   ....

(c) Do you agree that canoe sprint is really exciting to watch?

   Yes ☐   No ☐

(d) How likely are you to watch the canoe sprint event during London 2012?

   Likely ☐   Not very likely ☐

The wake produced by an object moving through the water is always the same shape. Whatever speed the object travels at, its wake always makes an angle of 39°.

Tim Brabants claims Gold for Great Britain in the 1000 m Kayak Sprint at the Beijing 2008 Games. As well as being an Olympic Gold-Medallist, Tim is a qualified doctor.

TWO-WAY TABLES

At the Beijing 2008 Games, Germany and Slovakia triumphed in the canoeing, winning 12 medals between them.

Germany won 3 Gold Medals and 3 Bronze Medals.

Slovakia won 4 medals in total, but none of them were Bronze.

Between them, the two countries won 3 Silver Medals.

1 This two-way table shows the medals won by each country.
Use the information above to complete the table.

		Gold	Silver	Bronze	Total
	Germany				
	Slovakia				
	Total				

2 How many Gold Medals did Slovakia win?

3 Germany chooses one of its Beijing 2008 canoeing medals at random.
Work out the probability that it is a Silver Medal.

The recommended daily intake of calories for adults is about 2500 for men and 2000 for women. During training, Tim Brabants consumes 5000-6000 calories every day because he is burning so much energy.

DESIGNING A QUESTIONNAIRE

Molly wants to find out how playing sports or exercising affects people's diets. She wants to know:

- how old each person is
- whether they play sports or exercise, and how much
- how many calories they consume each day
- what sorts of things they eat and drink before and after exercising.

1 Design a questionnaire for Molly to use. Include response boxes for at least one question.

2 Molly decides to carry out her survey at a local sports centre.
Give one reason why this might not be a good idea.

3 Explain how Molly could choose a random sample of students from her school to complete her survey.

HINT

You can include any extra questions you want to in your questionnaire.

MARATHON
PROBABILITY

NETWORK INFRASTRUCTURE

DID YOU KNOW? Cisco describes the reliability of its London 2012 network infrastructure as 'five-nines'. This means that the network is operational 99.999% of the time. At any given moment the probability of the network being unavailable is $\frac{1}{100\,000}$

CALCULATING PROBABILITIES

Here are some lettered tiles.

| M | A | R | A | T | H | O | N |

1 A tile is chosen at random. What is the probability that the tile shows

   HINT

   A, E, I, O and U are vowels.

   a a letter A

   b a vowel

   c a letter with reflection symmetry?

This pie chart gives information about the athletes who started the Men's Marathon at Beijing 2008.

72°

☐ Finished

☐ Did not finish

2 An athlete is chosen at random. What is the probability that the athlete

   a did not finish the marathon

   b finished the marathon?

3 How many of the 95 athletes who started the marathon did not finish?

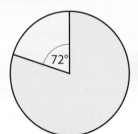

Comedian Eddie Izzard ran 43 marathons in 51 days in 2009. His 1100-mile journey raised £200 000 for charity.

British Paralympian David Weir won Gold at Beijing 2008 in the 800 m and the 1500 m. He won the 2011 London Marathon, finishing the 26.2-mile course in just an hour and a half.

INDEPENDENT EVENTS

At London 2012, the Women's Marathon takes place on 5 August and the Men's Marathon takes place on 12 August.

These calendars show the days it rained in London in August 2008 and August 2009.

AUGUST 2008						
SUN	MON	TUE	WED	THU	FRI	SAT
					1	R 2
R 3	4	R 5	6	7	8	R 9
R 10	R 11	R 12	R 13	14	15	16
R 17	18	19	R 20	R 21	22	R 23
24	25	26	27	28	29	R 30
R 31						

AUGUST 2009						
SUN	MON	TUE	WED	THU	FRI	SAT
						R 1
2	3	4	5	R 6	7	8
9	10	11	R 12	13	14	15
16	17	18	19	R 20	R 21	22
23	24	25	26	27	R 28	29
30	31					

① Use the data to estimate the probability that it will rain on any given day in August.

② Estimate the probability that it will rain on both marathon days.

③ Estimate the probability that it will not rain on either marathon day.

A marathon is 42 km long.

FIRST TO 42 km - A GAME FOR 2 PLAYERS

You will need two six-sided dice for Player 1 and two coins for Player 2.

Rules

Both players start on 0 km.

Player 1 rolls both dice and adds the total shown to their total of km.

Player 2 flips both coins:

- two heads: add 10 km to total
- one head and one tail: add 8 km to total
- two tails: add 6 km to total

Player 1 goes first. Then players take it in turns. The first player to reach 42 km or more is the winner.

① **a** Draw a table showing all the possible outcomes when 2 dice are rolled.

b What is the probability of getting a total of 10 or more?

② **a** Draw a table showing all the possible outcomes when 2 coins are flipped.

b What is the probability of getting 2 heads?

③ Who do you think is more likely to win 'First to 42 km'? Play the game with a partner 10 times. Record whether Player 1 wins or Player 2 wins. Estimate the probability that Player 1 wins the game.

HINT

You can combine your results with other students in your class to get a better estimate.

BMX

PYTHAGORAS' THEOREM

NETWORK INFRASTRUCTURE

DID YOU KNOW? The outdoor wireless network access points in the Olympic Park can operate at temperatures between −40 °C and 55 °C and in winds of up to 165 mph. 30% of the hardware in Cisco's network infrastructure will stay in place after the 2012 Games, to be used as part of London 2012's legacy.

After London 2012 the BMX Track will be open to the public.

FINDING MISSING LENGTHS

The diagram shows the starting ramp for the London 2012 BMX Track. The ramp is 8 m tall and can help riders reach speeds of up to 40 mph.

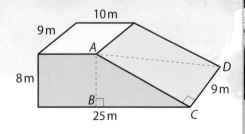

1   **a**   Work out the length BC.

    b   Work out the length of the sloping section of the ramp AC.

2   A support strut is placed diagonally across the ramp from A to D. Work out the length of the support strut. Give your answer in metres to 3 significant figures.

PROBLEM SOLVING WITH PYTHAGORAS

The diagram shows an Olympic BMX. The frame of the bike is made from lightweight aluminium. The frame has been highlighted in yellow.

1. Work out the total length of aluminium tubing needed to make the frame. Give your answer in cm to 3 significant figures.

2. Aluminium tubing weighs 800 g per metre. Work out the total mass of the frame in kg, to 3 significant figures.

To construct the BMX Track, engineers had to move enough soil to fill three Olympic Swimming Pools. The soil was taken from other parts of the Olympic Park, and was cleaned at a dedicated 'soil hospital'.

LENGTHS OF LINE SEGMENTS

The diagram shows part of a BMX track.
One side of each grid square represents 4 m.
A cyclist follows the red path around the track.

1. Work out the total distance the cyclist travels around the track. Give your answer in metres to 3 significant figures.

2. Plot your own path around the track.

   a. Use coordinates to describe your path.

   b. Work out the total length of your path. Can you find a path shorter than 150 m?

HINT

You can start anywhere on the START line and finish anywhere on the FINISH line. Your path must stay on the track at all times.

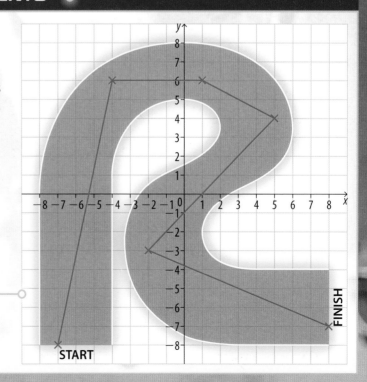

SYNCHRONISED SWIMMING

TRANSFORMATIONS

NETWORK INFRASTRUCTURE

DID YOU KNOW? Spectators watching the synchronised swimming events in the Aquatics Centre will be able to use Cisco's wireless hotspots to get online with their smartphones or tablets. Network infrastructure engineers use information from content providers to work out how much bandwidth they need to provide.

TRANSLATIONS

This diagram shows seven synchronised swimmers in a formation.

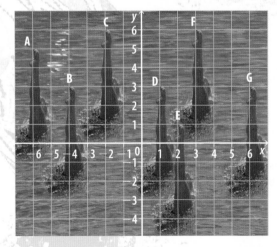

① Describe fully the transformation that maps

 a swimmer B onto swimmer C

 b swimmer G onto swimmer E.

② Swimmer E is translated using the vector $\begin{pmatrix} -1 \\ 2 \end{pmatrix}$. Which swimmer has she been mapped onto?

ROTATIONS AND REFLECTIONS

This synchronised swimming formation has rotation and reflection symmetry.

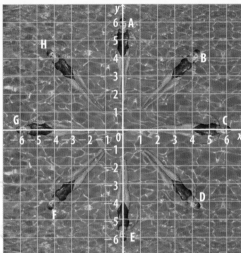

1. Describe fully a transformation which maps

   a   swimmer A onto swimmer C

   b   swimmer B onto swimmer H

   c   swimmer F onto swimmer E.

2. Describe fully two **different** transformations which map swimmer C onto swimmer G.

3. After a reflection, swimmer F is mapped onto swimmer B.
   Write down the equation of the mirror line.

4. Describe fully the rotation which maps swimmer D onto swimmer G.

DRAWING TRANSFORMATIONS

You have been challenged to design your own medal-winning formation for Great Britain's synchronised swimming team.

1. On a copy of the coordinate grid, reflect swimmer A in the line $x = 1$. Label the image B.

2. Rotate swimmer A 90° clockwise about the point (2, 0).
   Label the image C.

3. Use transformations to add at least three more swimmers to your formation. Label your swimmers with letters.
   Fully describe the transformation needed to map swimmer A onto each of your swimmers.

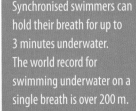

GYMNASTICS
SOLVING ANGLE PROBLEMS

NETWORK INFRASTRUCTURE

DID YOU KNOW? Cisco's network infrastructure will link the North Greenwich Arena to the Olympic Park. Cisco engineers estimate the maximum bandwidth necessary for critical voice and data communications. Then they provide double that amount, to make sure everything runs smoothly.

ANGLES IN PARALLEL LINES

This picture shows Chinese gymnast Li Xiaopeng on the parallel bars at the Beijing 2008 Games.

He went on to win the Gold Medal in this event.

1. Work out the size of angle x.
   Give a reason for your answer.

2. Work out the size of angle y.
   Give a reason for your answer.

3. Work out the size of angle z.
   Give a reason for each step of your working.

SOLVING ANGLE PROBLEMS

This vaulting horse is in the shape of a prism. Its cross-section is a trapezium. ADE is an isosceles triangle.

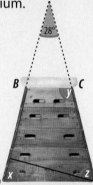

1. Calculate the size of angle x.
   Show all of your working.

2. Work out the size of angle y.
   Give a reason for each step of your working.

3. Calculate the size of angle z.
   Give a reason for each step of your working.

HINT

You can use these reasons in your answers:
- Alternate angles are equal
- Corresponding angles are equal
- Opposite angles are equal
- Angles in a triangle add up to 180°
- Angles on a straight line add up to 180°

The artistic gymnastics and trampoline events will take place at the North Greenwich Arena, formerly known as the Millennium Dome.

OLYMPIC HEROES

Louis Smith won Bronze for Great Britain in the Men's Pommel at Beijing 2008. He was the first British gymnast to win a medal at the Olympic Games since 1928.

ANGLES IN POLYGONS

The pylons supporting the North Greenwich Arena are placed at the vertices of a regular 12-sided polygon.

1. Work out the size of angle *x*. Show all of your working.

2. Work out the size of angle *y*. Show all of your working.

3. Work out the size of angle *z*. Show all of your working.

PARALYMPIC ROAD CYCLING
REAL-LIFE GRAPHS

NETWORK INFRASTRUCTURE

DID YOU KNOW? Brands Hatch is one of around 100 venues which will be linked using the London 2012 network. With cyber attacks on the increase, it's crucial that Cisco makes sure the network infrastructure is secure. Cryptographic keys protecting critical systems have 16^{32} combinations. Trying every combination would take billions of years, even using the most powerful computers in the world.

CONVERSION GRAPHS

There are 32 different road cycling events at the London 2012 Paralympic Games. Road races range from 30 km to 120 km and time trials range from 20 km to 35 km.

You can use this graph to convert km into miles.

① Use the graph to convert 20 km into miles.

② The road cycling track at Brands Hatch is approximately 4.8 miles long.
Use the graph to convert 4.8 miles into km.

③ Convert 120 km into miles.

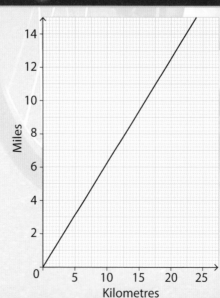

ON THE WEBSITE
Watch Rachel talk about her events, the Brands Hatch course, her training regime and her Olympic Gold Medal.

ON THE WEBSITE
Watch Rachel talk about the Brands Hatch course, the effect of weight on performance, her training regime and her Olympic Gold Medal.

Rachel Morris tests out the London 2012 road cycling course at Brands Hatch racetrack. She won Gold in the Women's Individual Time Trial at Beijing 2008.

DRAWING GRAPHS

Ben and Parminder want to try handcycling. They decide to compare two different companies that hire handcycles.

HENRY'S HANDCYCLES
£15 fixed rate for up to one hour
£10 per hour after the first hour

HANDCYCLE WORLD
Pay by the minute!
20p per minute

1. Draw a graph showing the cost of hiring a handcycle against time for each company. Use axes like these.

2. Ben and Parminder want to keep their handcycles for 3 hours. Use your graph to decide which company they should choose. Give a reason for your answer.

3. What is the length of time for which both companies would charge the same price?

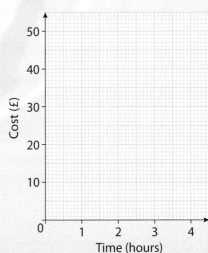

DISTANCE-TIME GRAPHS

Rachel is testing the Paralympic Course at Brands Hatch. The table shows the length of each section of the course and the time it takes her to complete it.

Section	Distance (km)	Time taken (s)
A → B	0.9	145
B → C	1.0	94
C → D	1.6	221
D → E	1.3	325
E → A	2.9	300

1. Draw a distance–time graph of Rachel's trip.

2. On which section of the course was Rachel travelling the slowest? Give a reason for your answer.

3. What was Rachel's average speed whilst going down Gorse Hill? Give your answer in km/h correct to 3 significant figures.

4. Calculate Rachel's average speed for the whole journey. Give your answer in km/h correct to 3 significant figures.

Paralympians ride hi-tech handcycles. Athletes use their hands to power the three-wheeled bikes. The event demands incredible upper body strength and stamina.

PENTATHLON
AVERAGES AND RANGE

NETWORK INFRASTRUCTURE

DID YOU KNOW? Cisco uses averages to describe how reliable a component is. By testing network infrastructure equipment in extreme conditions and gathering data from customers, network engineers can calculate the 'Mean Time Between Failures'. For the components in use at London 2012, this is about 200 000 hours.

AVERAGES FROM GROUPED DATA

In the fencing event, each pentathlete fights every other pentathlete once. In each bout, the competitors have one minute to score a single hit. If neither athlete scores a hit they both register a defeat. This table shows the number of wins the athletes scored in the women's fencing event in the Beijing 2008 pentathlon.

Number of wins	Frequency (f)	Midpoint (x)	f × x
0–4	1	2	
5–9	2		
10–14	6		
15–19	14		
20–24	11		
25–29	2		

1. How many athletes competed in total?
2. Write down the modal class interval.
3. Which class interval contains the median?
4. Copy and complete the table. Use your table to estimate the mean number of wins scored.

OLYMPIC HEROES

Britain's Heather Fell won Silver in the Women's Modern Pentathlon at the Beijing 2008 Games. She won 20 out of 35 of her fencing bouts.

In the modern pentathlon, athletes compete in running, shooting, fencing, swimming and horse riding.

COMPARING DATA

After the swimming event, pentathletes will have to travel from the Aquatics Centre to Greenwich Park to compete in the horse riding and combined running/shooting events.

Chris wants to work out the most reliable way to get from the Olympic Park to Greenwich. He asks a group of friends to try two different methods of transport and records their journey times in minutes:

| Train | 51 | 45 | 85 | 72 | 44 | | | |
| Cycling | 58 | 55 | 62 | 65 | 59 | 70 | 71 | 60 |

Compare fully the journey times for the two methods of transport.

HINT

You will need to calculate averages like the mean and median, and a measure of spread like the range. For each statistic you calculate, write a sentence comparing cycling to taking the train.

London 2012 organisers are aiming for 100% of spectators to get to the 2012 Games by public transport, walking or cycling.

CALCULATING THE MEAN FROM A FREQUENCY TABLE

A pentathlete is practising for the shooting event. She uses a specialised air pistol to aim at a target 10 m away. She can score 0, 2, 4, 6, 8 or 10 points on each shot. She records her results in a frequency table.

The athlete calculates that her mean score is 6.7. Unfortunately, she has accidentally shot a hole through one of her frequencies.

10m

Score	Frequency
0	1
2	1
4	2
6	6
8	🏶
10	4

The five events of the modern pentathlon were originally designed to simulate the challenges facing a military scout.

① Work out the missing frequency. Show all of your working.

② How many shots did the athlete fire in total?

ENERGY CENTRE

NUMBER SKILLS 2

One of the 60-tonne boilers in the London 2012 Energy Centre. Heat used in generating electricity will be captured and recycled to heat and cool the London 2012 venues.

NETWORK INFRASTRUCTURE

DID YOU KNOW? The London 2012 telephone network uses Cisco's 'Power over Ethernet' (PoE) technology. Instead of using separate transformers, power is delivered to each telephone through the same cable as the signal. This saves energy, helping to make London 2012 the greenest Olympic Games ever.

Over 130 km of overhead wires and 52 pylons were removed from the Olympic Park. Giant tunnels will allow power to be carried underground during the Games and in the future.

PERCENTAGE INCREASE AND DECREASE

1. The Energy Centre contains two hot water boilers weighing 60 tonnes each. When filled with water, the mass of the boilers will increase by 30%. Work out the mass of each boiler when filled with water.

2. At peak times during London 2012, the Olympic Park will require 37.1 MW of cooling power for air conditioning. The Energy Centre can supply 43% of this.

   a How much cooling power can the Energy Centre supply? Give your answer to the nearest MW.

   After London 2012, the amount of cooling power needed at peak times will reduce by 7.5%.

   b How much cooling power will be needed on the Olympic Park at peak times after London 2012? Give your answer in MW to 3 significant figures.

3. A primary substation will reduce the voltage of the generated electricity from 132 000 V to 11 000 V. Write this as a percentage decrease.

HINT

Power is a measure of how much energy something can deliver per second. It is measured in watts (W). A kilowatt (kW) is 1000 W. A megawatt (MW) is 1 000 000 W, or 1000 kW.

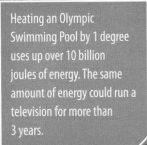

Heating an Olympic Swimming Pool by 1 degree uses up over 10 billion joules of energy. The same amount of energy could run a television for more than 3 years.

HINT

You will need to make assumptions about how many people watch each television set, and how many hours they watch for each day. Remember that the 2012 Games will last for 4 weeks.

ESTIMATION

About 2 billion people around the world will watch the London 2012 Games on television.
Here are some facts about CO_2 emissions from electrical appliances:

- A modern television uses about 0.1 kW of power, the same as a conventional lightbulb.
- If a 1 kW appliance runs for an hour it is responsible for about 0.5 kg of CO_2 emissions.

Use the information given to estimate the CO_2 emissions produced from people around the world watching London 2012 on television.
Write down any assumptions that you make.

SOLVING PERCENTAGE PROBLEMS

The London 2012 Energy Centre will use a technique of energy production called cogeneration. Instead of using a separate electricity generator and boiler, heat used to generate electricity will also be used to heat water and buildings. Cogeneration is a very efficient way of generating heat and power.

At peak times during the 2012 Games, the Olympic Park will need 74 MW of useful heat power.

Wood chip fuel costs £90 per tonne and contains 3 kWh of energy per kg.

A cubic metre of natural gas costs 40p and contains 11 kWh of energy.

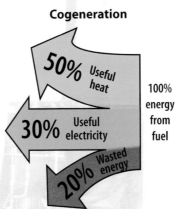

Cogeneration

50% Useful heat

30% Useful electricity

20% Wasted energy

100% energy from fuel

Conventional

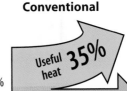

Useful heat 35%

Useful electricity 20%

Wasted energy 45%

1. Work out the cost of delivering an hour of peak heat requirements to the Olympic Park using
   a gas and cogeneration
   b gas and conventional power.
   Give your answers correct to 3 significant figures.

2. London 2012 has set a target for generating 20% of its power from renewable sources like sustainable wood chips. Work out the cost of the wood chips needed to deliver 20% of the peak heat requirement to the Olympic Park for one hour using cogeneration.

HINT

kWh stands for kilowatt-hour. It is the amount of energy used by a 1 kW appliance in 1 hour.

LEGACY AND SUSTAINABILITY
1 THE OLYMPIC STADIUM

NETWORK INFRASTRUCTURE

DID YOU KNOW? Cisco's reliable and efficient network infrastructure plays an important role in the sustainability of the 2012 Games. London 2012 organisers have used Cisco's lightning-fast network connections, IP telephones and video conferencing to stay in touch, reducing the need for air travel and reducing carbon emissions.

On these two pages you can see some of the innovations and decisions that helped make the London 2012 Olympic Stadium the most sustainable ever built.

Record breaking roof makes world records more likely

Engineer Tanya Ross talks about solving the problem: "You build a computer model and blow computer wind at it. It will tell you what the wind speed will be at any point inside the stadium."

Wind conditions can make a big difference to world record attempts. In the 100 m Sprint a following wind of more than 2 m/s would mean that no official world records could be set. And if the sprinters were running into a 2 m/s headwind they would find it very difficult to run record times.

The Olympic Stadium designers looked very carefully at how the shape of the stadium would affect wind speeds inside. Initial plans for the stadium didn't include a roof. But a powerful computer model showed that the roof could help reduce wind speeds inside the stadium, making world records more likely.

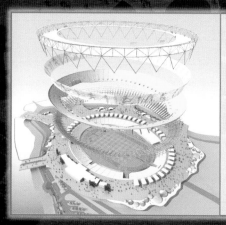

The stadium is part buried in the ground, with the field of play set as low as flood levels will permit. By incorporating the bottom 25 000 seats into the landscaping of the Olympic Park, the amount of steel required for the structure was drastically reduced.

The stadium roof is created from a network of steel cables, which reduces the amount of heavy, expensive steelwork required. The entire stadium only uses 10 000 tonnes of steel. This is less than 10% of the amount used for the Beijing 2008 stadium.

Some of the biggest steel tubes are made from reclaimed gas pipes.

ON THE WEBSITE
Watch the Olympic Stadium being built in a time-lapse sequence.

The external structure of the stadium will be covered by a temporary 'wrap', which is much lighter than traditional cladding. It will shelter spectators inside the stadium from the weather.

CHALLENGE 2012

PUT SUSTAINABILITY INTO PRACTICE BY PLANNING AN EVENT NEAR *YOUR* SCHOOL

Cisco is running a competition challenging schools to design a major sporting event in their area. To get involved, go to www.mathsandscience2012.co.uk/challenge2012 There is more information on page 11.

Saving water at London 2012

The 2012 Games are estimated to use 1 152 000 litres of water each day. Water usage is a very important consideration when constructing any sustainable building. Here are some of the measures used in the Olympic Stadium to reduce water usage.

- Dual-flush toilets using only 4.5 litres per flush
- Waterless urinals
- Low-flow showers with a maximum flow rate of 6 litres per minute
- Low-flow taps with a maximum flow rate of 0.08 litres per second

Maths Skills

1. Look at the information about toilets and water usage above. A traditional shower can use 15 litres of water per minute.

   a How much water would a traditional shower use during a 5-minute shower?

   b How much water would you save by using a low-flow shower with a maximum flow rate of 6 litres per minute?

2. The capacity of the Olympic Stadium is 80 000. During busy periods, about 30% of the people in the stadium might need to use a toilet. For every 12 people who need to use a toilet you should provide 1 toilet. 6% of the toilets provided should be accessible unisex toilets.

   How many accessible unisex toilets should be installed in the Olympic Stadium?

LEGACY AND SUSTAINABILITY
2 THE OLYMPIC PARK

NETWORK INFRASTRUCTURE

DID YOU KNOW? Up to 30% of the network infrastructure hardware Cisco will install on the Olympic Park will remain after the 2012 Games. This equipment will provide network connectivity for the thousands of future users of the Olympic Park, helping to contribute to the legacy of London 2012.

Sustainability is about more than just environmental responsibility and minimising waste. It means creating a 2012 Games which is accessible to a wide range of people of different backgrounds and abilities. It is about creating new employment and business opportunities, and providing a lasting legacy for the local area and beyond.

£1 billion Athletes' Village will be transformed after the 2012 Games

During London 2012 the Athletes' Village will provide accommodation for around 17 000 athletes and officials. The £1 billion development will be used after the 2012 Games to provide 2818 new homes for East London. Residents will benefit from the improved transport links created for the 2012 Games, new schools and utilities, and one of the largest urban parks built in Europe for 150 years.

ON THE WEBSITE
Watch videos showing the Olympic Park during the early stages of construction.

Olympic Park will be accessible for all

Up to 8% of spectators at London 2012 are expected to have difficulty negotiating stairs or escalators. With up to 20 000 mobility-impaired spectators a day visiting the Olympic Park during the 2012 Games, it is essential to consider how accessible the venues and facilities are. Engineers used cut-and-fill techniques to make sure the vast majority of the Park had no slopes steeper than 1 in 60.

In the five London boroughs adjoining the Park, at least 23% of the population require washing facilities before prayer. To meet the needs of different faith groups, at least one cubicle in each toilet block on the Olympic Park will contain a footbath with a spray hose.

This image is illustrative only and indicative of the aspirations for the future Park and should be viewed as such. It will be subject to change as plans for the Park and area develop over time.

The Olympic Park is at the heart of London 2012. The 150-acre site contains nine of the venues for the 2012 Games, including the Olympic Stadium, the Velodrome, the Aquatics Centre and the Basketball Arena.

Engineers built a 'soil hospital' to clean the site

Soil contamination was a huge issue on the Olympic Park. Tanneries, coal tar works and paint factories had all used the site, and the area had been a dumping ground for rubble after World War Two bombings.

In order to reuse soil from the site, a 'soil hospital' was set up. A set of 50-tonne machines washed, sieved and shook contamination out of the soil. Tar, cyanide, petrol and lead were all removed. The cleaned soil was tested to make sure it was safe, and then reused on the Olympic Park.

Transforming the lives of people throughout the UK

Promoting healthy living is an important part of creating a sustainable 2012 Games. The creation of 50 km of new cycle routes and 30 km of new walking routes will improve access to and around the Olympic Park. With nearly three-quarters of car journeys in the UK being less than five miles, walking and cycling are ideal ways of saving time and money whilst exercising.

The London 2012 Changing Places programme encourages volunteers to carry out projects to improve their local communities. The projects are centred on the host boroughs, and include creating new habitats for birds and bats and planting trees.

Over 30 000 jobs will be created during construction for London 2012, including at least 350 apprenticeships. During the 2012 Games more than 100 000 people will be employed in jobs including catering, cleaning and security.

Maths Skills

1. Around 800 000 m³ of contaminated soil was cleaned in the 'soil hospital' on the Olympic Park.

   a The density of soil is 1500 kg/m³. Calculate the total mass of soil which was cleaned in the 'soil hospital'.

   b Convert 800 000 m³ into km³.

2. Cut-and-fill is a way of levelling areas of ground. Soil from raised areas is moved into lower lying areas. Work out whether the area of soil **A** will completely fill the holes at **B** and **C**. Show all of your working.

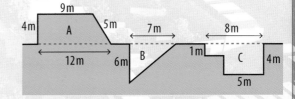

TRANSFORMING YOUR FUTURE

1 QUALIFICATIONS IN MATHS AND SCIENCE

Without the maths and science skills of thousands of engineers, architects, project managers, sports scientists, accountants, lawyers, technicians, builders and IT experts, the London 2012 Olympic and Paralympic Games could never exist.

Maths and science are everywhere, from the food you eat and the clothes you wear, to the software that lets you check your email or text your friends.

Qualifications in maths and science can open the door to more exciting jobs and higher salaries. They can also give you a leg-up when you're looking for a university or college place.

Maths and science qualifications can give you more choices when looking for jobs or university or college places.

Why study maths and science post-16?

✓ **Get a head start in other subjects**
Economics, ICT, sports science and geography all use maths and science.

✓ **Impress admissions tutors**
Whichever subject you apply for at university or college, an A-level or Higher in maths or science will help you stand out from the crowd.

✓ **Land a great job**
Science helps you develop communication and team-working skills that will impress potential employers.

✓ **Earn more**
Graduates and non-graduates who have an A-level or Higher in maths tend to earn more than those of similar ability and background who don't.

✓ **Increase your options**
With a qualification in maths or science you're likely to have more choice at university or college, and when you're looking for a job.

✓ **Learn to solve problems**
Science and maths are all about understanding how the world works and using that knowledge to solve problems.

POST-16 SPOTLIGHT: MATHS

Students study algebra, geometry and calculus as well as options from statistics, mechanics and decision maths. Decision maths has lots of applications in computer programming. And you can use mechanics to work out how fast a roller coaster needs to travel to keep everyone in their seats!

POST-16 SPOTLIGHT: PHYSICS

Physics students get hands-on with radioactivity, electricity and magnetism. You can build electric motors, use lasers and learn how particle accelerators work, recreating experiments which inspired well-known physicists like Professor Brian Cox.

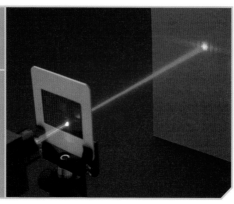

Cisco Networking Academy

The Cisco Networking Academy is a global education programme which teaches students how to design, build, troubleshoot and secure computer networks. Students complete hands-on learning activities and network simulations to develop the practical skills needed for ICT and networking careers in virtually every type of industry. Students also develop essential workplace skills such as problem-solving, collaboration and critical thinking.

There are more than 350 schools, universities and colleges in the UK which offer courses from the Cisco Networking Academy, giving students an opportunity to develop ICT literacy skills, and work towards future careers in IT or networking.

Visit http://cisco.netacad.net for more information.

POST-16 SPOTLIGHT: CHEMISTRY

Chemistry is the study of matter. Chemistry gives us clean water, medicines and technologies like flat-screen televisions. Chemistry students learn about the atomic structures of molecules, finding out how chemical reactions in a car's catalytic converter can help to reduce harmful emissions.

POST-16 SPOTLIGHT: BIOLOGY

Biology students learn about the building blocks of life, and how genetics and stem-cell research are shaping the future of medicine. Studying biology is a crucial step to becoming a doctor, dentist, nurse or vet, and can also lead to careers in agriculture, psychology, robotics, forensic science and physiotherapy.

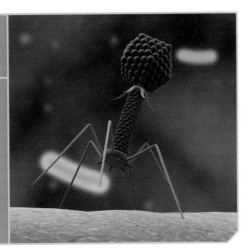

PROFILE: DAVID KONOPEK
THE SYSTEMS ANALYST

Technology enthusiast David Konopek turned to the Cisco Networking Academy when he decided he was interested in a career in ICT. "Networking skills are in demand throughout the world," says David, "and people who are Cisco certified don't worry too much about getting a job."

Through the Academy, David earned his Cisco Certified Networking Associate qualification. "It was a great mix of theory and practical experience that was highly stimulating," he recalls.

After graduating, David had the know-how and confidence he needed to start his own business. David's working life offers a great deal of variety and flexibility, thanks to a wide range of skills and experience – and he is currently taking steps to expand his qualifications. "Now I am building up my own business," he says. "I have also enrolled in a distance-learning university programme, in order to obtain a bachelor's degree in Business ICT." David plans to return to the Cisco Networking Academy to complete a more advanced qualification in the future.

TRANSFORMING YOUR FUTURE

2 CAREERS IN MATHS AND SCIENCE

The world we live in is changing. The internet has transformed the way we live, work and communicate. People are living longer and moving more freely between countries. And our climate may be changing too.

To seize the opportunities and solve the problems associated with these changes, there is a need for people with maths and science skills: engineers, chemists, doctors, computer scientists, physicists and countless others who will all contribute to the world's future.

Training in maths and science will help you play your part, and these fundamental skills will give you the flexibility to explore different careers throughout your life.

Old technologies are still creating some of our planet's greatest problems. *New* technologies will help solve them.

ON THE WEBSITE
Watch Tim Brabants talk about his medical career and success at Beijing 2008.

PROFILE: TIM BRABANTS
OLYMPIC GOLD MEDALLIST AND MEDICAL DOCTOR

Weeks after winning a Gold Medal in the Men's 1000 m Kayak event at Beijing 2008, qualified medical doctor Tim Brabants returned to his job in A&E at Queen's Medical Centre in Nottingham.

After getting three As at A-level Tim chose to study at the University of Nottingham, which has a great reputation for medicine as well as fantastic kayaking facilities. "Medicine and sport have a lot in common," says Tim. "As a doctor, I work in a team."

Tim has taken a break from life as a doctor, taking advantage of help from sponsors like Cisco to focus his efforts on London 2012.

He was awarded an MBE in 2009.

PROFILE: CECILIA BAGENHOLM
BUILDING DOCTOR

Cecilia Bagenholm is a senior consultant at the engineering company Buro Happold. She makes sure that Buro Happold's engineering projects meet environmental standards and don't have a negative impact on plant and animal life.

Maths and science skills opened up a huge range of careers, and it was environmental issues that Cecilia chose. Maths and science A-levels led to a degree in civil engineering at Imperial College, London. This was followed by an MSc in environmental technology and a career working around the world to develop standards for environmentally-friendly houses.

ON THE WEBSITE
Watch Richard Kruse talk about London 2012 both as an engineer and a medal hope.

PROFILE: RICHARD KRUSE
OLYMPIC FENCER AND ENGINEER

Richard Kruse is Britain's most successful fencer in almost 50 years, and has already competed in two Olympic Games. He is also a qualified civil engineer.

Richard completed his degree at City University in London in the same year that he represented Team GB in the Athens 2004 Games. "Fencing and engineering both require a logical mind," says Richard.

While working for engineering company Buro Happold, Richard contributed to the design of the Olympic Park. "I worked on accessibility for the disabled, making sure there are enough rest stops," he says. Richard plans to make the most of his home advantage in the foil event at London 2012.

Transforming technologies

As the world's population increases, the demands we make on resources and the environment increase. Scientists are constantly working to develop new solutions for everything from generating electrical power to recycling waste materials. With skills in maths and science you could play a crucial role in developing technologies and ideas which will help future generations. *What will your legacy be?*

Maths and science in the 21st century

RENEWABLE ENERGY

To reduce our reliance on dwindling supplies of polluting fuels, such as oil, gas and coal, we need to develop renewable energy technologies. This solar power plant uses mirrors shaped like a quadratic curve to reflect sunlight on to a tube of heat-absorbing fluid.

▶ **ON THE WEBSITE**
Watch Ellen MacArthur talk about her career transformation from sailor to campaigner.

PROFILE: ELLEN MACARTHUR
ROUND-THE-WORLD YACHTSWOMAN NOW INSPIRING RE-THINKING AND RE-DESIGN

Ellen MacArthur first hit the headlines in 2001 when she secured second place in the Vendée Globe round-the-world sailing race at the age of only 24. She went on to become the fastest person to circumnavigate the globe single-handed, when in 2005 she sailed around the world in just 71 days and 14 hours.

She is a founder of the Ellen MacArthur Trust, set up in 2003, a charity which takes young people recovering from cancer and other serious illnesses sailing. She was knighted by the Queen in 2005, and following four years of research and having spent time working with government and key industry sectors, she retired from professional sailing to set up the Ellen MacArthur Foundation. The Foundation links education and business to inspire young people to re-think and re-design their future through the vision of a circular economy.

Turn the page to find out more about the circular economy, and how it could help you in the Maths and Science Challenge 2012.

QUANTUM COMPUTING

Mathematicians and computer scientists are learning how to use strange quantum properties of subatomic particles to make lightning-fast computers. Modern encryption is based on prime numbers and factorisation. It would take thousands of years to factorise a 300-digit number using a conventional computer. A quantum computer could do it in seconds, making most modern codes useless.

FLEXIBLE E-PAPER

Can you imagine a world without paper? Engineers and scientists are developing flexible screens which you can roll up and carry in your pocket. These light, low-powered displays could replace computers, printers and paper in the near future.

www.mathsandscience2012.co.uk

Go online to watch these videos and find out more about careers in maths and science.

LAST WORD... THE CIRCULAR ECONOMY

WHAT IS IT AND HOW WILL IT HELP US?

Designing systems

The circular economy is based on the understanding that systems can repair and restore themselves. In these systems, materials and energy flow endlessly without being wasted. For example, trees in a forest drop dead leaves, and these leaves provide nutrition for fungi and bacteria. The fungi and bacteria nourish the soil and the soil then nourishes the tree. So the system has changed the tree's waste into food that it can use.

These systems have a positive impact. Designers are now beginning to use these insights to design man-made products, materials and even cities to have a similar positive impact.

BIOMIMICRY'S COOL ALTERNATIVE: EASTGATE CENTRE IN HARARE

The Eastgate Centre in Harare is Zimbabwe's largest office and shopping complex. The building was designed by architect Mick Pearce and is one of the best examples of biomimicry – solving human problems by examining nature. It has no conventional air conditioning or heating, yet keeps a regular temperature all year round using very little energy.

It achieves this by mimicking the self-cooling mounds of African termites. Termite mounds include small tunnels that enable hot air from the main chambers below ground to be drawn up by the breeze. The hot air flows up through the mound and is released through vents at the top. The termites can regulate the temperature by opening or blocking the tunnels to control air flow. A similar method is used in the Eastgate Centre, as can be seen by the chimneys that line its roof.

CHALLENGE 2012

GIVE YOUR VENUE A POSITIVE IMPACT

Turn waste into 'food'

Materials should never be thrown away or become waste. Materials need to be designed so that when they are no longer needed in their current use, they can provide 'food' for the next cycle.

This can be achieved in two ways. One option is to create materials that can decompose safely, and so nourish the soil. The alternative is to create materials that can be re-used again and again, circulating from business to business.

Think in systems

How do things connect and flow? What are all the consequences of our decisions? These are the questions we should be asking ourselves if we want to work in systems. As Zimbabwe's Eastgate Centre shows, nature can provide a lot of the answers.

Shift to renewables

Fossil fuels are running out. It is essential that we move to renewable energies such as wind, solar and tidal. This has already started, but we still have a long way to go.

ON THE WEBSITE
Watch this short animation explaining the circular economy.

ON THE WEBSITE
Watch Ellen MacArthur introduce the Maths and Science Challenge 2012, and explain how this thinking can help your project.